Making
GREAT
SCRAPBOOK PAGES

Its Easier Than You Think

PAGE DESIGNERS

We are grateful to the following people for creating the album pages which appear in this book. Some of these designers work for manufacturers who supply products for memory albums, and some have scrapbooking retail stores (see page 144). We're proud to feature their wonderful album pages. In alphabetical order, they are:

- **Brenda Birrell** for Pebbles in My Pocket
- **Nancy Church** for Pebbles in My Pocket
- **Sandi Genovese** for Ellison® Craft & Design
- **LeNae Gerig** for Hot Off The Press, Inc.
- **Becky Goughnour** for Hot Off The Press, Inc.
- **Katie Hacker** for Hot Off The Press, Inc.
- **Debbie Hewitt**, Agoura, California
- **Joy Huish** for Pebbles in My Pocket
- **Allison Meyers** for Memory Lane
- **Launa Naylor** for Pebbles in My Pocket
- **Debbie Peterson**, Kennewick, Washington
- **Susan Shea** for Hot Off The Press, Inc.
- **Kathy Slack**, Lomita, California
- **Ann Smith** for Memory Lane
- **Anne-Marie Spencer** for Hot Off The Press, Inc.
- **Stephanie Taylor**, Valencia, California

published by:

HOT OFF THE PRESS INC.

©1998 by **HOT OFF THE PRESS** INC. All rights reserved. No part of this publication may be reproduced or utilized in any form or by any means, including photocopying, without permission in writing from the publisher. Printed in the United States of America.

The information in this book is presented in good faith; however, no warranty is given nor are results guaranteed. Hot Off The Press, Inc. disclaims any liability for untoward results.

The designs in this book are protected by copyright; however, you may make the designs for your personal use or to sell for pin money. This use has been surpassed when the designs are made by employees or sold through commercial outlets. Not for commercial reproduction.

Warning: Extreme care must be exercised whenever using a glue gun, as burns may result. Never leave a child unattended with a glue gun.

Hot Off The Press wants to be kind to the environment. Whenever possible we follow the 3 R's—reduce, reuse and recycle. We use soy and UV inks that greatly reduce the release of volatile organic solvents.

For a color catalog of nearly 300 craft books, send $2.00 to:

HOT OFF THE PRESS INC.
1250 N.W. Third, Dept. B
Canby, Oregon 97013
phone (503) 266-9102
fax (503) 266-8749
http://www.hotp.com

Hot Off The Press dedicates this book to the memory of our colleague and dear friend, Joe Peterson: 1975–1998. He will be missed.

PRODUCTION CREDITS

Project editor	Mary Margaret Hite
Photographer	Kevin Laubacher
Graphic designers	Sally Clarke
	Jacie Pete
	Susan Shea
Digital imagers	Victoria Gleason
	Larry Seith
Editors	Lynda Hill
	Paulette Jarvey
	Tom Muir

Making

GREAT
SCRAPBOOK PAGES

It's Easier Than You Think

- 230 album pages
- over 15 techniques
- 13 journaling styles
- guidelines, hints & tips

TABLE OF CONTENTS

All About Scrapbooking

We each have a story to tell and memories to save. Making memory albums or scrapbooking gives us the opportunity to do both. It's all about getting those precious photos out of shoe boxes and into albums where they can be seen and shared. Best of all, no experience or expertise is necessary. You'll use paper, scissors and glue. It's as simple as cutting and gluing. There are all sorts of special tools and products which are nice to have but paper, scissors and glue are the basics.

It's important to use acid-free and lignin-free papers, plus acid-free glues and acid-free pens. Acid-free products have a neutral pH factor and will not cause further deterioration of your photos (terms are defined on page 143). We believe it's also important to keep this activity manageable and enjoyable. Begin with your most recent photos and, as you can, work back in time. If you try to start with your birth or marriage, the task will soon become overwhelming then you'll push those shoe boxes back in the closet and miss out on all the fun! The most important thing is to take the time—even just one hour a week—to work on your scrapbooks. You might want to join a friend or relative and work on your albums together to share the fun.

To make it easier for you to reproduce the techniques in this book, the products used are listed next to each album page. Paper Pizazz™ is available in book form and by the sheet, although not every pattern is sold by the sheet. We've listed the book title, in italics— for instance, *Childhood* or *Pretty Papers*. Then, if the specific paper is available by the sheet, we'll also give its name in parentheses: *Christmas* (snowflakes).

This chapter's background paper is from
Paper Pizazz™ Bright Great Backgrounds.

PLAIN PAGE

BETTER PAGE

PAGE WITH PIZAZZ!

This book is designed to offer guidelines (we hesitate to call them rules) and lots of examples to help you make your album pages wonderful. Learning about focal points, mixing shapes, varying sizes, overlapping elements and coordinating papers will give you the tools to turn plain pages into fun, clever or pretty album pages. Then we'll move into page techniques like offset matting, splitting a page, 2-for-1, clever corners, shadowing, quilting and more to add to your design tool kit.

Look at the album pages above and below to see how the plain pages are improved by cropping and matting the photos (shown in more detail on pages 10–11). The better pages have a die-cut sun or flower stickers added as embellishments. However, the pages have

pizazz when patterned background papers are added. The papers work two ways: (1) by mirroring the action as with the red wagon or (2) by picking up a color in the photos as with the yellow hearts paper, which matches the overalls. The pages with pizazz become more alive in your album and better reflect the personality or action in your photos.

You may choose to make every page one with pizazz, or every second page, or third page. We believe an album full of only "better" pages can be somewhat boring. The goal of this book is to give you the tools to easily create the best scrapbook pages possible—quickly, too.

What must you have?
❏ acid-free adhesive
❏ acid-free black pen

❏ straight-edged scissors
❏ pattern-edged scissors
❏ acid-free plain papers
❏ acid-free patterned papers
❏ plastic templates—circle, oval, heart, star
❏ album or 3-ring binder
❏ acid-free sheet protectors (to match your album size)

What's nice to have? Stickers, die cuts, paper doilies, more patterned papers (all acid-free and lignin-free, of course), punches, corner punches and scissors, red-eye pen (to remove red eye in flash photos), pet eye pen (same thing for pet photos), patterned rulers, stencils, more templates, more pattern-edged scissors, rubber stamps—and more comes on the market every day!

PLAIN PAGE

BETTER PAGE

PAGE WITH PIZAZZ!

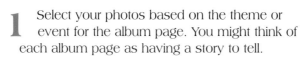

1 Select your photos based on the theme or event for the album page. You might think of each album page as having a story to tell.

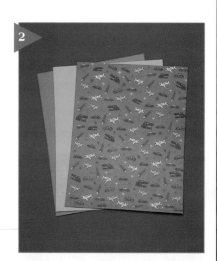

2 Select plain and patterned papers to complement your photos. You might find a themed patterned paper that will mirror the story of your photos. Then choose colors to coordinate with the patterned paper. Or, as shown at the bottom of page 8, you may simply want to choose patterned papers with colors to complement your photos.

3 Crop your photos (more about this on page 10). Here a plastic template helps make a perfect oval.

4 Mat your photos with plain or patterned paper (page 11 goes into more detail about matting). Glue the cropped photos to the paper and cut ⅛"–½" away using plain or pattern-edged scissors.

5 Arrange the photos—pages 14 and 15 will offer some guidelines. Here we've mixed sizes and shapes for a pleasing arrangement.

6 Add decorative elements—punches, stickers, die cuts, etc. This banner and airplanes are die cuts ©Ellison® Craft & Design.

7 Lastly you journal. This is where you add words to finish your page's story. Keep it as brief or as involved as you think is necessary. We've journaled on the die cuts as well as on the mat around the silhouetted photo. Now slip the completed page into a sheet protector, then into your album.

CROPPING—think of it as clever cutting

Yes, you can cut photos or, if you're nervous, cut a color copy. Cropping photos allows you to get more photos per page and to make your pages more interesting.

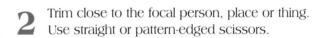

1 Leave historical items like houses, cars or furniture—they'll be fun to see years from now.

2 Trim close to the focal person, place or thing. Use straight or pattern-edged scissors.

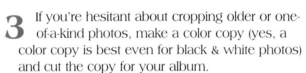

3 If you're hesitant about cropping older or one-of-a-kind photos, make a color copy (yes, a color copy is best even for black & white photos) and cut the copy for your album.

4 Use a plastic template for smooth ovals, perfect circles and great shapes. Place the template on top of the photo and draw a line on the photo. Then cut inside the line. Lots of shapes are available.

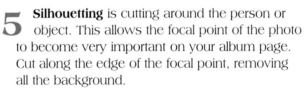

5 **Silhouetting** is cutting around the person or object. This allows the focal point of the photo to become very important on your album page. Cut along the edge of the focal point, removing all the background.

6 **Bumping out** one section of the photo is silhouetting one area, but leaving the rest of the photo with a background. This cropping technique works especially well with balloons or elbows.

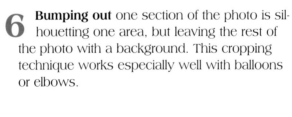

7 Yes, Polaroid photos can be cropped, just do not cut into the white envelope at the bottom of the photo. For freshly-developed photos, wait 10–15 minutes until they are completely dry before cropping.

Matting

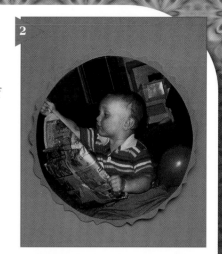

1 Glue the cut-out (cropped) photo to a sheet of paper and cut ⅛"–½" away, forming a mat. Use plain or patterned paper for the mat. Use straight-edged scissors...

2 ...or pattern-edged scissors for one or both cuts. It's fun to mix and match cuts.

3 When matting a bumped-out cropped photo, it's good to keep the mat simple and cut close to the photo.

4 Double mat some photos, varying the sizes of the mats from narrow to wide.

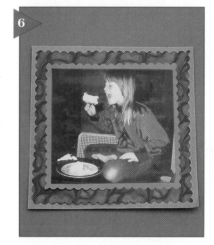

5 Mix straight-edged and pattern-edged scissors on your photos and mats.

6 How about a triple mat, just for fun? Or quadruple mat, or more?

7 Mix your mat shapes, perhaps putting an oval inside a rectangle.

8 And journaling on a wide mat offers a great look!

Gosh, They're Bright!

"Won't those bright papers overwhelm my photos?" novice scrapbookers always ask. "Not unless you let them!" we answer. The most vivid patterns will be broken up and subdued by the photographs, mats and decorative elements you place on your page. The trick is to choose coordinated papers and to be a little daring! Paper Pizazz™ papers have been designed to work together, and we'll help you with the daring part.

The two papers below are very bright—by themselves, the stripes could make you dizzy! But look how well they work together on this page.

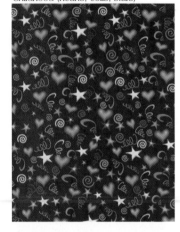

Childhood (hearts, coils, stars)

Birthday (colorful stripes)

The corrugated paper patterns on these papers have muted colors, but the patterns are very strong and dominant. Still, when they're combined with matted photos and journaling, they complement the photos rather than calling attention to themselves.

Country (blue corrugated)

Country (brown corrugated)

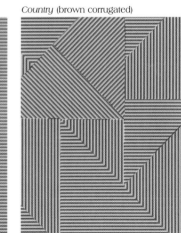

6-10-95 Congrats, Wendy!

Graduation is an exciting time, colorfully reflected by this patterned paper. With matted photos, Wendy the graduate takes center stage, wonderfully framed by the bright paper.

Teen Years (graduation caps)

WAY TO GO ERIK!

ONE WAY

OUR NEW DRIVER 8-5-97

Becoming a first time driver is a scary if exhilarating time. Both patterned papers are perfect compliments to the theme but these road signs are sure bright! However, with the more muted map paper as photo matting, the road signs paper becomes a terrific background to Erik's big day!

Vacation (road signs)

Vacation (road map)

13

A Few Rules

1 ESTABLISH A FOCAL POINT:

Throughout this book you will find references to the "focal point" of a page. The focal point is simply that item on a page which draws your eye. A page without a clear focal point lacks impact and may be confusing. All three photos at left are darling—but choosing and enlarging one gives the page a focus.

Paper Pizazz™: *Birthday* (lines & dots)
Glasses die cuts: Ellison® Craft & Design

2 VARY SIZES:

Mix photo sizes for interest; enlarge a photo or two if needed. The left page photos are all the same size, while one is enlarged for the right page. What a difference!

Paper Pizazz™: *School Days* (school tartan, cork board, yellow pad)

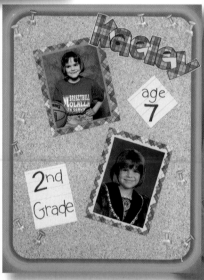

3 VARY SHAPES:

Even with a clear focal point and a variety of sizes, a page can be bland if the elements are too similar. The four ovals on the left page are—well, boring. The right-hand page, with its mixture of oval, round and rectangular mats, is a big improvement. Triangular corners add yet another shape and pull your eye around the page.

Paper Pizazz™: *Country* (wire & daisies)

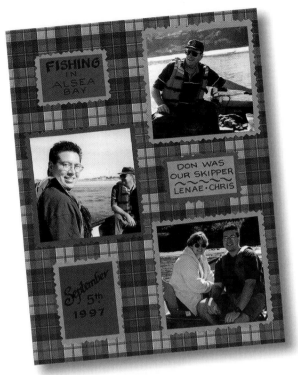

4 OVERLAP ELEMENTS:

More photos will fit on a page with room for journaling if you overlap photos and other elements. The left page is nice, but becomes more interesting when the photos are simply overlapped. Overlapping also makes room for the fish and pole which beautifully frame the page and turns a page of rectangular shapes into a more interesting album page.

Paper Pizazz™: *Great Outdoors* (brown plaid)
Fish, pole cutouts: *Paper Pizazz™ Great Outdoors*

5 DIRECT THE VIEWER'S EYE:

As a rule, we "read" a page following a figure Z. By creating a focal point and placing photos along the Z, you control the order in which the page is viewed while drawing the eye through your album page. In this page the eye first sees the center photo of Jake, which is why silhouetting that photo makes good sense. Then the eye darts from "Oh, goody!" to "Tasty box!" to "Jake" to "Got one!" to "So Yummy!" A great page and fun to see! The busy animal crackers patterned paper only reinforces the theme of Jake snacking and does not overwhelm his photos.

Paper Pizazz™: *Child's Play* (animal crackers)

Tips for Terrific Photos

◄ Take lots of shots, never just one! Some will turn out better than others.

➤ Take the same scene from different distances and angles—(1) far away; (2) closer; (3) up close & personal!

◄ Include ACTION in your photos.

◄ When taking "set-up" or posed shots, have people do more than just smile at the camera. Ham it up! A good picture is interesting even if you don't know the people in it.

10-Minute Pages

People often are afraid to get involved in crafting memory albums because "it takes too long." It's true that some complex, intricate pages may take an hour or more to do—but your pages don't have to be that difficult. Making album pages should be a fun way to capture memories for the future; don't turn it into a chore!

You can spend as much or as little time as you want on a given page. Most of the pages in your album should take only 5–10 minutes to complete. You may want to spend more time on some special photos or memories of a special time, but many photos almost speak for themselves. (Just don't leave out the important details of when and where.)

Once the photos and papers were chosen, this page took only five minutes to complete. The focal photo, themed paper and cutouts give the basic story; the remaining photos and journaling tell us the "how."

Paper Pizazz™: *Childhood* (Ouch!)
Bandaid cutouts: *Paper Pizazz™ Childhood*
Decorative scissors: pinking by Fiskars®, Inc.

A combination background and double-matted photos made the page on the left a little more time-consuming, but it still took only ten minutes to create.

Paper Pizazz™: *Solid Muted Colors, Bright Great Backgrounds*
Decorative scissors: deckle by Fiskars®, Inc.

Coordinating Papers & Pages

The four album pages shown on this page and page 19 illustrate how papers can be combined and coordinated in different ways to create many different looks.

Using the black, white and red colors of the photo as a starting point, a red paper with white polka dots was selected to coordinate with white and black solid colors. The polka dot theme was reinforced with punched circles: black ones to make polka dots on the white mat, white ones to spell the subject's name, smaller red dots to embellish the lettering.

Paper Pizazz™: *Ho Ho Ho* (white dot on red)
Circle punches: Fiskars®, Inc.
Decorative scissors: scallop by Fiskars®, Inc.
Page designer: LeNae Gerig for Hot Off The Press, Inc.

The same polka dot paper used on the page above gets a more festive feel in this page. Here it's combined with a red/white striped paper and solids in bright primary colors, chosen to match the birthday boy's clothing.

Paper Pizazz™: *Ho Ho Ho* (white dot on red, red & white stripes)
Stickers: Frances Meyer, Inc.®
Decorative scissors: pinking by Fiskars®, Inc.
Page designer: LeNae Gerig for Hot Off The Press, Inc.

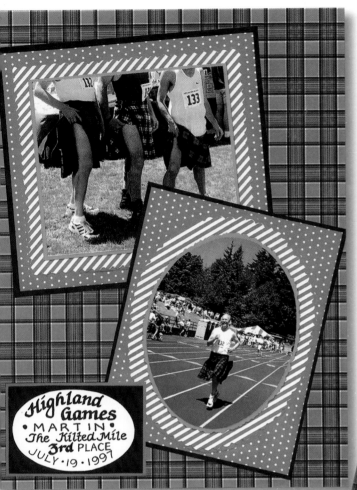

You might think adding yet another patterned paper would make a page far too busy, but the green plaid background used for the highland games photos actually "tones down" this page while reinforcing the Scottish theme. The page also has four solid colors—red, green, black and white—for a total of seven papers on this one page. Since the solids accent and coordinate with the plaid, the total effect is discreet and rich.

Paper Pizazz™: *Ho Ho Ho* (white dot on red, red & white stripes, green plaid)
Decorative scissors: deckle, scallop by Fiskars®, Inc.
Page designer: Becky Goughnour for Hot Off The Press, Inc.

A narrow red mat separates the pine tree paper from the plaid paper and picks up the colors of the inner mats. This page also uses seven different papers, four patterns and three solids, but avoids a cluttered look by having a clear focal point and a coordinated plan.

Paper Pizazz™: *Ho Ho Ho* (white dot on red, red & white stripe, green plaid), *Vacation* (pine trees)
Stickers: ©Mrs. Grossman's Paper Company
Decorative scissors: volcano by Fiskars®, Inc.
Page designer: LeNae Gerig for Hot Off The Press, Inc.

The four album pages shown on this page and page 21 all use the same three patterned papers, yet each album page is different, not only in subject but in mood.

Pretty Papers (purple sponged) *Wedding* (white satin) *Pretty Papers* (hydrangeas)

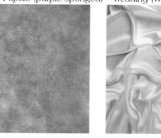

A formal page suits a wedding. The white satin paper was matted in a muted purple solid and centered on the hydrangea paper so the hydrangeas form a subtly patterned border. ¼" wide stripes cut from a brighter violet solid create an inner border. The group portrait was triple matted with a wider center mat to produce the effect of a framed photo, then mounted slightly off-center to accommodate the heart-shaped portrait of the bride and groom. A smaller heart matted to match the heart photo was used for journaling.

Heart template: Déjà Views™ by C-Thru® Ruler Co.
Page designer: Becky Goughnour for Hot Off The Press, Inc.

To start this page, the hydrangea paper was cut apart with two wavy vertical lines 6" apart. The center piece was mounted on the sponged paper with the hydrangea edges ½" away on each side. The satin paper provides just a touch of texture for the photo mats.

Decorative scissors: colonial by Fiskars®, Inc.
Alphabet stickers: Frances Meyer, Inc.®
Decorative ruler: Déjà Views™ by C-Thru® Ruler Co.
Page designer: LeNae Gerig for Hot Off The Press, Inc.

enjoying the beauty in our back yard~

~Summer 1997

Here two of the three patterned papers are trimmed into smaller rectangles, then aligned at the top right to create a two-sided frame with a casual feel. The matted photos bump out of the frame to accentuate the informality of the arrangement.

Decorative scissors: ripple, seagull by Fiskars®, Inc.
Calligraphy pen: Zig® by EK Success Ltd.
Page designer: Becky Goughnour for Hot Off The Press, Inc.

This very simple arrangement (a "five-minute page") is created with layered mats of different widths. The diagonal rectangle of hydrangea paper breaks up the regularity of the centered mats to keep the page from appearing overly formal. Notice how the black-and-white photo is beautifully framed with colorful patterned papers.

Decorative scissors: colonial by Fiskars®, Inc.
Page designer: LeNae Gerig for Hot Off The Press, Inc.

Theme Pages

You establish a theme, or central idea, for your page simply by choosing related photos. By keeping that idea in mind as you choose patterned and plain papers, you reinforce the theme and increase the impact of your photos.

The cookie background is an obvious choice for these baking photos. Plain paper, cut into circles and decorated with punched "chips," provides an appropriate space for journaling, and the baking equipment stickers relate to the action. As a clever touch, the upper cookie was "nibbled" with decorative scissors.

Paper Pizazz™: *Child's Play* (chocolate chip)
¼" round punch: McGill, Inc.
Stickers: Stickopotamus™ by EK Success Ltd.
Decorative scissors: deckle by Fiskars®, Inc.
Page designer: LeNae Gerig for Hot Off The Press, Inc.

The interlocking blocks on the background paper are a natural match for the interlocking alphabet in the photos. Another view of the birthday boy is tied into the previous photos by matting it on a solid paper notched to match the blocks and stepping stones.

Paper Pizazz™: *Quick & Easy*
Page designer: Allison
   Meyers for
   Memory Lane

These wedding photos have a garden setting, so what could be more natural than to frame them with a garden lattice paper embellished with leaf stickers? We love the lattice cut to make a frame! The roses of the background paper, even though a different color, echo the roses of the bride's bouquet.

Paper Pizazz™: *Wedding* (muted roses, lattice)
Stickers: ©Mrs. Grossman's Paper Company
Decorative scissors: deckle by Fiskars®, Inc.
Page designer: Debbie Peterson

Sometimes photos with no obvious relationship can be linked by designing a theme page around them. Crop each photo to a 2½" square and double-mat them to resemble building blocks. Stack them in a triangle and place them on a paper printed with baby blocks. The alphabet squares and journaling block further the theme.

Paper Pizazz™: *Child's Play* (blocks & dots)
Square punch: Family Treasures
Page designer: Allison Meyers for Memory Lane

Use a die-cutting machine to make your own die-cut shapes to go with your photos. Patterned autumn leaf paper and two coordinating solid colors were cut into the maple leaf shape, then all were "piled" on this page.

Paper Pizazz™: *Country* (burlap), *Holidays & Seasons* (autumn leaves)
Maple leaf die cuts: Ellison® Craft & Design
Metallic gold pen: Zig® by EK Success Ltd.
Decorative scissors: volcano by Fiskars®, Inc.
Page designer: LeNae Gerig for Hot Off The Press, Inc.

You can also draw and cut out your own shapes to suit your page. The water theme of this page begins with the photos and raindrop paper. The hose and the aqua "puddle" for the journaling were cut from solid papers (the hose pattern is on page 138). The top left photo was also cut in a splashy freehand shape. Splash stickers complete the themed look.

Paper Pizazz™: *Child's Play* (raindrops)
Stickers: Frances Meyer, Inc.®
Page designer: Allison Meyers for Memory Lane

A whimsical American flag echoes the flag proudly waved by the little star of this patriotic page.

Paper Pizazz™: *Adult Birthday* (blue stars), *Ho Ho Ho* (red & white stripes)
Star punches: McGill, Inc.
Metallic silver pen: Marvy® Uchida
Page designer: LeNae Gerig for Hot Off The Press, Inc.

After the parade Daddy carried me home!

Everyone loves a pun! The caption for this page links the two most popular elements of Halloween, the "corny" costumes and the trick-or-treat candy. Candy corn background paper, candy corn stickers and larger candies cut from plain paper all tie into the theme.

Paper Pizazz™: *Holidays & Seasons* (candy corn)
Candy corn stickers: Stickopotamus™ by EK Success Ltd.
Page designer: Allison Meyers for Memory Lane

...just a little bit "CORNY!"

...Halloween 1996...

Scary Skeleton!

Let's Split!

We've defined three techniques to add interest to your album pages, and all of them use cut-apart or split paper. Offset matting is simply turning the mat at a different angle than the photo. Sound simple? It is! But it gives a great look as shown with the beach photos on page 29. And turning the background paper like an offset mat adds even more interest, as shown on pages 28–29. Like many of the techniques in this book, once you know it you'll probably find all sorts of uses for it in your memory albums.

Next is shadowing; that is, to make a paper shadow. Like offset matting, this technique is all about cutting and placing paper. To make a shadow just cut around the item, then place the shadow so it extends on 1–2 sides of the item (like a real shadow would). Shadowing is effective in several ways: shadowing silhouetted photos like those of Regina on page 30, shadowing mats as seen on the Siamese cat album page above Regina, shadowing die cuts like the camera on page 31, shadowing cutouts like the frogs on page 31 and the cat and mouse on page 30. There are many ways to do shadowing!

Splitting a page can also be done in a variety of ways—with a decorative ruler as on page 32 or with long, even wainscoting-like splits on page 33 provide an elegant look. Use pattern-edged scissors for some splits (top of page 34, bottom of 36, bottom of 37), or use straight scissors for your splits. On the top of page 36 the designer split the page, then matted the splits. As you'll see, splits can be even or uneven, balanced or not, and they can follow the design in the Paper Pizazz™ or (you guessed it!) not! Splitting is another easy-to-use technique that once you know, you'll find lots of opportunities to use.

This chapter's background paper is from *Paper Pizazz™ Light Great Backgrounds*.

Offset Mats

A mat doesn't have to be an even border all around the edge of a photo, and a background paper doesn't have to sit straight on the page. Offsetting one or more mats and background papers adds interest to your pages.

An offset mat can emphasize an especially rich paper. The music staffs are an appropriate choice for the band photos, and the metallic tones complement the brass instruments. First the photos were double-matted, then an offset mat in a coordinating solid metallic was added behind each. The background mat is matted and set at an angle on the dotted sheet.

Paper Pizazz™: *Metallic Papers*
Saxaphone die cut: Ellison® Craft & Design
Page designer: LeNae Gerig for Hot Off The Press, Inc.

Offset mats and offset backgrounds create a swirl of colors that reflect Emerald's tie-dyed shirt.

Paper Pizazz™: *Bright Great Backgrounds*
Crayon punch-outs: *Paper Pizazz™ School Punch-Outs™*
Alphabet stickers: Making Memories™
Page designer: LeNae Gerig for Hot Off The Press, Inc.

Scallop-edged red mats are set over diagonal offset double mats to tie together the rectangular and star-shaped photos. A clever border of punched footprints wanders across the edge of the background sheet, keeping the page from looking **too** regular and formal.

Paper Pizazz™: *Disney's Holidays & Seasons with Mickey & Friends*
Footprint punch: Marvy® Uchida
Star template: Provo Craft®
Decorative scissors: mini scallop by Fiskars®, Inc.
Page designer: Becky Goughnour for Hot Off The Press, Inc.

A ⅝" wide pink mat provides an area for journaling, then a narrow black mat is slightly offset to balance the effect of the Minnie Mouse sheet, which is placed diagonally on the pink background—a simple offset mat. The photo corners are a perfect finishing touch, picking up the black from the mat and Brinsley's dress.

Paper Pizazz™: *Disney's Playtime with Mickey & Friends*
Corners: Fiskars® Corner Edgers
Page designer: LeNae Gerig for Hot Off The Press, Inc.

Shadowing

"Shadowing" is creating a mat which matches the shape of the matted item, then placing it offset behind the shape. To get a true shadow effect, it's important to place the mats in the same relative position for each element, as though each is lighted from the same source.

To shadow an irregular shape such as the cat or mouse, lay the matted shape upside down on the wrong side of the shadow color. Trace it lightly, then cut around the pencil line and turn the mat over.

Paper Pizazz™: *Pets* (pet prints), *Bright Great Backgrounds*
Circle, rounded rectangle templates: Déjà Views by C-Thru® Ruler Co.
Page designer: Susan Shea for Hot Off The Press, Inc.

Compare this page to the one above—here the light comes from the lower right, so the shadows are offset to the top and left. Soft colors and a grassy background echo the photos.

Paper Pizazz™: *Pets* (grass), *Solid Muted Colors*
Decorative scissors: deckle by Fiskars®, Inc.
Page designer: Becky Goughnour for Hot Off The Press, Inc.

Regina & Chris' African pygmy hedgehog. He got her for Christmas 1996. Here is the "huntress" stalking her prey in the savanna.

REGINA

You can also shadow only one element on a page to give it a three-dimensional effect. Here only the camera is shadowed (the camera pattern is on page 138).

Paper Pizazz™: *Vacation* (film strips)
Camera die cut: Ellison® Craft & Design
Page designer: LeNae Gerig for Hot Off The
   Press, Inc.

Rather than blending into the background, these frogs hop right off the page!

Paper Pizazz™: *Great Outdoors* (camping
   equipment)
Frog cutouts: *Paper Pizazz™ Child's Play*
Decorative scissors: bow tie by Fiskars®, Inc.
Corner rounders: Family Treasures
Page designer: Katie Hacker for Hot Off The
   Press, Inc.

Splitting a Page

Interesting effects are achieved by cutting a page apart, then putting it back together on another sheet.

Simple and special! Three rectangles of "sponged"-patterned paper are cut, then mounted ⅜" apart on a plain white sheet. The three split areas become frames for photos and provide room for journaling. The purple moiré accents and white mats serve to tie the groups together.

Paper Pizazz™: *Pretty Papers* (purple moiré, purple sponged)
Decorative scissors: deckle by Fiskars®, Inc.
Page designer: Debbie Peterson

Using a patterned ruler for a scalloped edge design, 1½" strips were cut down each long edge of the teapot paper. These strips were matted on bright yellow solid paper, then used as borders for the plaid background paper.

Paper Pizazz™: *Child's Play* (teapots & dolls), *Light Great Backgrounds*
Heart template: Provo Craft®
Decorative scissors: scallop by Fiskars®, Inc.
Scalloped ruler: Déjà Views™ by C-Thru® Ruler Co.
Page designer: Becky Goughnour for Hot Off The Press, Inc.

The designer calls these splits "wainscoting." Cut 1" wide straight strips of patterned paper and mount them ⅛" apart—trim the outside strips if necessary to make them fit. Here the rose paper was mounted on a pastel pink. The page, the photos and the text block were then matted on ivory to pick up the sepia tone of the photos. Some of the photo elements were subtly handcolored.

Paper Pizazz™: *Wedding* (muted roses)
Handcoloring pens: SpotPen™
Photo mounting corners: Canson®
Border punch: McGill, Inc.
Page designer: Allison Meyers for Memory Lane

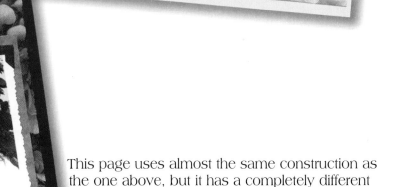

This page uses almost the same construction as the one above, but it has a completely different look due to the choice of papers.

Paper Pizazz™: *Pretty Papers* (hydrangea, purple sponged)
Decorative scissors: deckle edge by Family Treasures
Corner cuts: Fiskars® Corner Edgers
Photo mounting corners: Canson®
Page designer: Allison Meyers for Memory Lane

This page was split by cutting it apart following the lines of the rivers on the patterned paper, then mounting it on a deeper blue solid. The cut areas provide journaling room. Wavy scissors enhance the watery effect. The clever frame around the "Russell Family Reunion" sign is made of ½" paper strips with simple hand-drawn woodgrain features.

Paper Pizazz™: *Great Outdoors* (paddling)
Decorative scissors: wave by Fiskars®, Inc.
Page designer: LeNae Gerig for Hot Off The Press, Inc.

The smooth curves splitting this page are reminiscent of a beach and provide an anchor for the shell cutouts.

Paper Pizazz™: *Vacation*
Shell cutouts: *Paper Pizazz™ Embellishments*
Decorative scissors: zipper by Fiskars®, Inc.
Page designer: LeNae Gerig for Hot Off The Press, Inc.

Even splits: 1" strips of patterned paper are cut, then glued 1" apart on a coordinating solid color. The dotted paper makes festive mats.

Paper Pizazz™: *Ho Ho Ho* (red & green dots), *Christmas* (Christmas candy)
Stickers: ©Mrs. Grossman's Paper Company
Page designer: Allison Meyers for Memory Lane

2" wide stripes cut from a solid red paper are mounted diagonally on the plaid background paper. The black photo mats pick up the subtle black stripe on the plaid paper. Who says plaids and stripes don't mix?

Paper Pizazz™: *Ho Ho Ho* (red & white stripes, green plaid)
Bow punch: Family Treasures
Page designer: Allison Meyers for Memory Lane

An evenly split page: Two-section rows of plaid paper were cut and matted on red, then placed horizontally ⅝" apart on black paper to make a striking background for these hiking photos. The photos bump out above and below the plaid strips, and the silver lettering really stands out on the black background. Great page splitting!

Paper Pizazz™: *Great Outdoors* (red/black plaid)
Red & silver pens: Zig™ by EK Success Ltd.
Decorative scissors: deckle by Fiskars®, Inc.
Page designer: Becky Goughnour for Hot Off The Press, Inc.

Here are diagonal splits created with 1½" wide diagonal stripes of baseball paper placed ⅜" apart on a solid red background. Note how your eye follows the action in the photos, getting successively closer until it ends up at the larger posed foreground shot.

Paper Pizazz™: *Sports* (baseballs)
Baseball, mitt, cap cutouts: *Paper Pizazz™ Sports*
Red & silver pens: Zig™ by EK Success Ltd.
Decorative scissors: ripple by Fiskars®, Inc.
Page designer: LeNae Gerig for Hot Off The Press, Inc.

Irregular splits: These follow the rows of bugs on the background paper with irregular, wavy strips. They were glued ½"–1" apart to this solid green page, suggesting the wandering paths pursued by Zack in his bug hunt.

Paper Pizazz™: *Child's Play* (friendly bugs)
Frog, butterfly cutouts: *Paper Pizazz™ Child's Play*
Decorative scissors: scallop by Fiskars®, Inc.
Page designer: LeNae Gerig for Hot Off The Press, Inc.

Uneven splits are made using wave scissors to create the effect of an ocean reef with ripples lapping the beach—a wonderful imaginary location for Garrett's swim.

Paper Pizazz™: *Vacation* (fish)
Fish cutouts: *Paper Pizazz™ Vacation Punch-Outs™*
Decorative scissors: wave by Fiskars®, Inc.
Page designer: Ann Smith for Memory Lane

Double-Page Spreads

Often we work on album pages one at a time, and it's easy to forget that when your album is open the pages will be viewed as a spread of two pages. This chapter shows examples of pages that were designed to be seen together.

On pages 40-43 there are eight spreads—each uses only one sheet of patterned Paper Pizazz™, so we call this a 2-for-1 technique. Now, we know patterned papers are inexpensive, but it proved a fun challenge to these designers and the spreads have the added benefit that they certainly "go" together.

Because Paper Pizazz™ books of papers are designed to coordinate, it's easy to create spreads with a theme like the country reunion on page 44 and the football spread on page 46. Using the middle of the two-page spread as the focal point is effec tivley demonstrated by designer Katie Hacker's spreads on pages 46–47. Sometimes a double-page spread of background Paper Pizazz™ seems to be generic; that is, it can be used for many photo memories. For example, see the layout at the bottom of page 45. The spread at the top of page 44 and the top of 45 use Paper Pizazz™ to reinforce the theme of the pages, a perfect use for a single album page and even better on a double-page spread.

This chapter's background paper is from
Paper Pizazz™ Light Great Backgrounds.

2 for 1

Use one piece of paper to make two coordinating pages—this not only creates a coordinated look, but makes more economical use of special papers.

Go-together pages don't need to have duplicate layouts; the only matching element on these is the rounded gold background. Using the center of the road signs paper from the left page as a mat on the right page ties these two together.

Paper Pizazz™: *Vacation* (road signs)
Alphabet stickers: Making Memories™
Sign stickers: Frances Meyer, Inc.®
Decorative scissors: peaks by Fiskars®, Inc.
Page designer: Ann Smith for Memory Lane

The center section of the star paper from the right page makes the offset mat on the left page. The small stars were cut using a template, then the large stars and moon were drawn freehand in a similar style (patterns are on page 139).

Paper Pizazz™: *Adult Birthday* (blue stars)
Small star, moon, banner templates: Provo Cra
Silver pen: Marvy® Uchida
Decorative Scissors: deckle by Fiskars®, Inc.
Page designer: Allison Meyers for Memory Lane

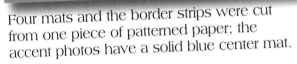

Four mats and the border strips were cut from one piece of patterned paper; the accent photos have a solid blue center mat.

Paper Pizazz™: *Childhood* (ABC blocks)
Blocks cutout: *Paper Pizazz™ Childhood*
Decorative scissors: scallop by Fiskars®, Inc.
Page designer: Becky Goughnour for Hot Off The Press, Inc.

Here one patterned paper was cut into ten horizontal strips. Five were used on each page to create a continuous pattern across both. Different solid colors were used for each mat, with all the colors taken from the silhouette paper for a consistent look.

Paper Pizazz™: *Childhood* (small kid silhouette, large kid silhouette)
Decorative scissors: deckle by Fiskars®, Inc.
Page designer: LeNae Gerig for Hot Off The Press, Inc.

Matted strips from a patterned sheet border the outside edges of these pages, bringing the focus to the inside. The pumpkins (actually orange apples) used for journaling are arranged to draw your eye across the spread.

Paper Pizazz™: *Holidays & Seasons* (candy corn)
Apple punch: Marvy® Uchida
Bat die cuts: Ellison® Craft & Design

Decorative scissors: volcano by Fiskars®, Inc.
Green, yellow paint markers: Marvy® Uchida
Page designers: LeNae Gerig & Becky Goughnour for Hot Off The Press, Inc.

© & ™ Ellison® Craft & Design

Carefully cut the center from a patterned page, then mount it on a coordinating solid. Glue the leftover border on a matching solid page to create two different but coordinated backgrounds.

Paper Pizazz™: *Bright Great Backgrounds*
Frog cutout: *Paper Pizazz™ Child's Play*
Dinousaur cutout: *Paper Pizazz™ Childhood*
Alphabet stickers: Making Memories™
Photo corners: Frances Meyer, Inc.®
Page designer: LeNae Gerig for Hot Off The Press, Inc.

Best Friends

Amanda

Kaeley

AMANDA AND KAELEY, BEST FRIENDS SINCE THEY WERE TODDLERS

APRIL 1997

A 2" strip was cut from each edge of the Flounder paper. The center section was mounted on the center of a plain page and the edges on the sides of a matching plain page to create a reverse-image pair. The beach balls were cut from plain papers to echo the balls in the photos.

Paper Pizazz™: *Disney's The Little Mermaid*
Alphabet stickers: Making Memories™
Decorative edge ruler: Déjà Views® by C-Thru® Ruler Co.
Decorative scissors: ripple by Fiskars®, Inc.
Page designer: LeNae Gerig for Hot Off The Press, Inc.

Sometimes the simplest approach works best, especially when the page elements are very colorful. Six ⅝" horizontal strips were cut from the dotted paper and mounted on two sheets of solid yellow. The same paper was used to mat one photo on each page.

Paper Pizazz™: *Ho Ho Ho* (white dot on red)
Mickey Mouse cutouts: *Disney's Playtime with Mickey & Friends*
Camera cutout: *Paper Pizazz™ Vacation*
Bow punch: McGill, Inc.
Decorative scissors: ripple by Fiskars®, Inc.
Gold pen: Marvy® Uchida
Page designer: LeNae Gerig for Hot Off The Press, Inc.

June 1992
Our trip to Disneyland

The Peterson FAMILY

HAPPY TIMES AT DISNEYLAND • DAVE AND GOOFY SHARE A HUG AND A SMILE

43

More 2-page Spreads

Except for the first and last, every page in your album is opposite another page! Take advantage of this to create larger thematic groupings.

Not all photos have to fit completely on the page, as shown above. Notice the journaling block at the top, which was typed on acid-free paper and matted to match the photos.

Paper Pizazz™: *Great Outdoors* (moose & deer)
Tree punch: McGill, Inc.
Computer typeface: D.J. Inkers™
Page designer: Launa Naylor for Pebbles in My Pocket

The pages below are not the same, but they share a theme and color scheme. Cutting photos and text to fit inside elements such as the barn doors and silo is one of the quickest, easiest ways to put a page together.

Paper Pizazz™: *Country* (barn, barnwood)
Small barn cutout: *Paper Pizazz™ Country*
Decorative scissors: deckle by Fiskars®, Inc.
Page designer: LeNae Gerig for Hot Off The Press, Inc.

Treat two pages as if they were one page with a continuous border around both. Text and graphics read across the center line.

Paper Pizazz™: *Child's Play* (friendly bugs)
Insect stickers: ©Mrs. Grossman's Paper Company
Alphabet die cuts: Accu/Cut® Systems
Page designer: Allison Meyers for Memory Lane

The same paper was used for the background of both pages, and another paper was used across the middle of the spread. ⅝" strips of different solid colors border the center section. The border colors were also used for the mats and text blocks to mute the brightness of the backgrounds.

Paper Pizazz™: *Bright Great Backgrounds*
Decorative scissors: jigsaw by Fiskars®, Inc.
Page designer: Katie Hacker for Hot Off The Press, Inc.

Borrowing the 2-for-1 technique, the large photo on the left was matted on the cut-out center from the right page. Cropping two photos in a football shape not only fits the page theme but allows them to be more easily angled and overlapped to fill the page.

Paper Pizazz™: *Sports* (footballs, football field)
Football cutouts: *Paper Pizazz™ Sports*
Decorative scissors: deckle by Fiskars®, Inc.

Silver pen: Marvy® Uchida
Page designer: Becky Goughnour for Hot Off The Press, Inc.

Sometimes the photos are an embellishment to the pages rather than the other way around. Here the large map and the extensive journaling tell the whole story; the photos of Katie and Craig, the loaded car and the new home add a personal touch.

Paper Pizazz™: *Vacation* (road map, road signs), *Teen Years* (blue jeans)
Sign cutouts: *Paper Pizazz™ Vacation*
Star punch: Marvy® Uchida
Decorative scissors: ripple by Fiskars®, Inc.
Page designer: Katie Hacker for Hot Off The Press, Inc.

Inside the image (handwritten notes):

Art was everywhere!

Being at Harlaxton opened my mind to the possibilities.

Built in 1837, this English manor now houses the University of Evansville's British Campus. The semester of 1994 was really incredible (.)

HARLAXTON COLLEGE, UK

When I arrived, I couldn't believe my eyes!

My home and school for four months.

Like the map on page 46, the large British flag spread across both pages immediately tells the viewer what's happening. Subtle patterns and solids in the same red-white-and-blue scheme are effective but not too dominant for mats and backgrounds.

Paper Pizazz™: *Wedding* (white satin), *Bright Great Backgrounds*
Decorative scissors: colonial by Fiskars®, Inc.
Page designer: Katie Hacker for Hot Off The Press, Inc.

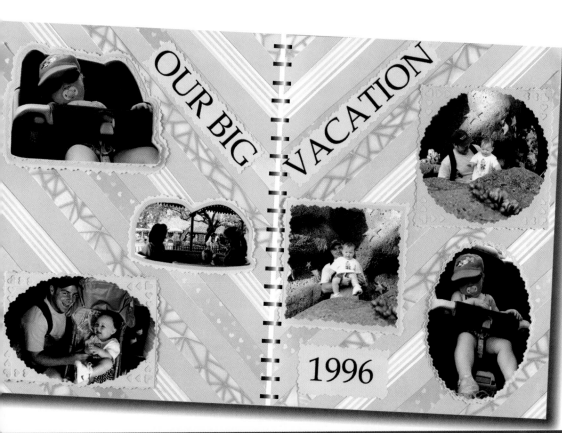

Inside the image:

OUR BIG VACATION

1996

A very effective spread is created by cutting 1" wide stripes of patterned papers and mounting them in opposite diagonals, forming a mirror image. The headline also follows the V shape across the two pages.

Paper Pizazz™: *Baby* (pastel stripes, pastel hearts, pastel quilt)
Decorative scissors: ripple by Fiskars®, Inc.
Heart corner punch: McGill, Inc.
Page designer: Anne-Marie Spencer for Hot Off The Press, Inc.

Corners & Borders & Rulers, Oh My!

Making easy yet creative borders and corners can be the difference between an average album page and one with pizazz! And you know how we like pizazz-y pages!! Sometimes you only have a couple of photos, yet the event is worthy of a whole album page dedicated to it. With creative corners and borders, these pages will look full and be attractive, too.

Borders can easily be made of stickers, die cuts or paper punched shapes, and you'll find examples in this chapter. You can draw borders with a fine-tip pen (see the top of page 53) or journal on a wide border (top of 54). Paper strips make great borders (see page 56) and using hand punches will make a lacy border as shown at the bottom of page 57. Borders can be embossed (page 58) or created with paper and pen to match the theme of the photos (see the top of page 60).

Decorative corners can be made with corner edger scissors and corner punches—tools specifically designed for making corners. These scissors are used on the tops of pages 51 and 59. Corner punches can be seen at the bottom of page 47 and on page 128. Beautiful corners can be made with Paper Pizazz™ as shown on page 50—and see page 53 for western corners made with barnwood Paper Pizazz™ (we suspect colorful corners could be made out of other Pizazz™ designs). You can also make corners with strips of paper as demonstrated at the bottoms of pages 55 and 59.

Rulers make great borders and corners. There are rulers designed especially for memory albums and some 8½"x11" templates have decorative rulers on the edges. Rulers make elegant corners when used on plain or patterned Paper Pizazz™. They look great when matted on one side (as shown on the top of page 51) or matted on all sides (top of page 50). Using a ruler and drawing directly on the album page gives lots of options especially when embellished with stickers (like the border on the bottom of page 52 and the corners on the bottom of page 60). Cutting strips of Paper Pizazz™ using a ruler, then wrapping the strips around each other makes a unique border as you can see at the bottom of page 51. The album pages on page 61 show a ruler used on the edges of Paper Pizazz™ to make an all-around border or two clever corners. Lots of choices and lots of examples in this chapter to add to your creative tool kit!

This chapter's background paper is from
Paper Pizazz™ Bright Great Backgrounds.

The lace corners are the perfect finishing touch for this wedding page done in sepia tones. A template was used to cut the corners from a lace-patterned paper, then each corner was double-matted on brown and ivory. The arched shape of the corners echoes the shape of the scissors used on the photo mats and lace background paper.

Paper Pizazz™: *Black & White Photos* (crushed suede)
Corner template: border corner arch by Keeping Memories Alive™
Decorative scissors: majestic by Fiskars®, Inc.
Page designer: Debbie Peterson

A stunning laser-cut paper lace forms the corners for this page. The diagonal lines of the background complement the angled photos and are softened by the curves of the paper lace and the decorative scissors used on the tone-on-tone ivory mats.

Paper Pizazz™: *Romantic Papers*
Laser-cut Lace: *Paper Pizazz™ Romantic Papers*
Decorative scissors: colonial by Fiskars®, Inc.
Page designer: LeNae Gerig for Hot Off The Press, Inc.

A special portrait gets a lush treatment in this lavishly layered page inspired by the floral design of Laura's dress. The photo itself was simply rounded on each corner, then double-matted on similarly rounded mats. The photo was centered on the flowered background paper, then triple corners were cut using a decorative ruler to create soft scallops. Roses cut from the background paper adorn the corners and nameplate.

Paper Pizazz™: *Romantic Papers*
Decorative ruler: Déjà Views™ by C-Thru® Ruler Co.
Corner cutter: rounder by Fiskars®, Inc.
Decorative scissors: colonial by Fiskars®, Inc.
Page designer: Katie Hacker for Hot Off The Press, Inc.

Creative use of scallop scissors and a wavy ruler helped create this clever page. Use the ruler to trace lines ⅜" apart on the solid paper; repeat with patterned paper (it's easier if you trace on the back of the sheet). Cut out, then weave the strips together as shown to make a border. Each daisy begins with a 2" circle. Trim with scallop scissors, then cut each scallop ¾" toward the center. The daisy centers are ¾" yellow circles trimmed with a deckle edge and dotted with a black pen.

Paper Pizazz™: *Country* (wire & daisies)
Decorative ruler: Déjà Views™ by C-Thru® Ruler Co.
Decorative scissors: scallop, mini-scallop, deckle by Fiskars®, Inc.
Page designer: Debbie Peterson

51

EDITE · 9 MONTHS · HE'S ALL SMILES · FROM HIS HEAD TO HIS TOES · SMILES · FROM HIS HEAD TO HIS TOES · EDDIE · 9 MONTHS · HE'S ALL

photograph ©Sears Photo Studio

It's serendipitous when you find elements that go together like this! The paint-splattered paper reflects the paint-splattered background of the photo, and the stickers are a perfect echo of the paper. The border was created by applying stickers to plain yellow paper, positioning them to extend under the matted photo. The yellow mat was trimmed to clip off the ends of some stickers so they seem to completely fill the border. A single sticker in the corner of the photo brings your eye inward.

Paper Pizazz™: *School Days* (splats)
Splat stickers: Frances Meyer, Inc.®
Decorative scissors: bow tie by Fiskars®, Inc.
Page designer: LeNae Gerig for Hot Off The Press, Inc.

A wavy ruler was used to draw parallel lines to frame this page. The stickers add depth to the border and repeat elements from the background paper for a unified appearance.

Paper Pizazz™: *Book of Firsts*
Decorative ruler: Déjà Views™ by C-Thru® Ruler Co.
Decorative scissors: volcano by Fiskars®, Inc.
Pumpkin, candy corn, rope, bat stickers: ©Mrs. Grossman's Paper Co.
Page designer: Debbie Peterson

·Amber·Y·Tara·Derek·Megan·

This border gets a sense of movement from simple line drawings done with a fine-point pen. The snowflakes were punched around the edge of a white paper first, then it was matted on navy to match the snowflake paper. After the photos were placed, the pen was used to add motion lines, dots and tiny snowflakes to the border.

Paper Pizazz™: *Holidays & Seasons*
Snowflake punch: Marvy® Uchida
Page designer: Ann Smith for Memory Lane

An asymmetrical border adds interest to a page. This one was created by trimming 1½" off the left side and bottom of the burlap paper, matting it on solid green which shows only on the trimmed edges, then mounting it on the barnwood paper with the top right corners aligned. A section of barnwood was matted on green and mounted diagonally across the corner. Note the double mat on the photo—the inner green mat connects the photo to the page, while the outer purple mat picks up the color of the girls' shirts. Stickers matted in the same colors relate to the cowgirl theme.

Paper Pizazz™: *Country* (barnwood, burlap)
Western stickers: Frances Meyer, Inc.®
Page designer: LeNae Gerig for Hot Off The Press, Inc.

A wide border can be useful for journaling—in this case, a whimsical comment on the nature of outdoor eating, also reflected in the paper choice and the large die-cut ant. The border paper was chosen to match the color of the hot dog bun and placed off-center to balance the bun.

Paper Pizazz™: *Great Outdoors* (picnic ants)
Decorative scissors: bow tie by Fiskars®, Inc.
Ant die cut: Ellison® Craft & Design
Page designer: LeNae Gerig for Hot Off The Press, Inc.

Make a posed photo more festive with a bright border of layered die cuts. The balloons, noisemakers and confetti were cut from solid colors chosen to match the background dots. (The noisemaker patterns are on page 140.)

Paper Pizazz™: *Bright Great Backgrounds*
Die cuts: Ellison® Craft & Design
Page designer: LeNae Gerig for Hot Off The Press, Inc.

all dies © & ™
Ellison® Craft
& Design

The top and bottom borders of this page were made by cutting 1⅜" wide strips of the plaid paper, gluing them to a solid black paper and using the same scissors to trim 1/16" away on each side. The narrow black edging exactly follows the scalloped line. The same technique was used for the photo mats.

Paper Pizazz™: *Country* (denim), *Ho Ho Ho* (Christmas plaid)
Decorative scissors: seagull by Fiskars®, Inc.
Cow stickers: Frances Meyer, Inc.®
Red, white paint pens: Zig® by EK Success Ltd.
Page designer: LeNae Gerig for Hot Off The Press, Inc.

Betty's a black-and-white cat, but there is plenty of color in her page—from the background felines to the criss-crossed border strips to the double-matted photos (each in a different color combination). Note that each sticker letter was also matted in a different rainbow color.

Paper Pizazz™: *Pets* (colorful cats)
Decorative scissors: jigsaw by Fiskars®, Inc.
Corner rounder: Family Treasures
Alphabet stickers: Making Memories™
Page designer: Katie Hacker for Hot Off The Press, Inc.

A simple paper strip border acquires pizazz when it's matted on a contrasting shade. Here ⅜" wide dotted strips were mounted on black. The mat was trimmed with decorative scissors, which were turned over to cut a mirror-image pattern on the opposite side of the strip. Setting the strips in from the edge of the background paper makes the border seem wider.

Paper Pizazz™: *Ho Ho Ho* (white dot on red)
Decorative scissors: bubbles by Fiskars®, Inc.
Red pen: Zig® by EK Success Ltd.
Page designer: Becky Goughnour for Hot Off The Press, Inc.

Borders can be balanced without being symmetrical. Here a double border of ¼" wide paper strips set ¼" apart is used to define two areas on the background paper. A balancing border at the left and bottom of the page is created by offsetting the background paper on a pink solid.

Paper Pizazz™: *Baby* (pastel dots, pastel quilt)
Heart template: Extra Special Products
Decorative scissors: colonial by Fiskars®, Inc.
Page designer: Katie Hacker for Hot Off The Press, Inc.

Creating a border with punches allows you to use the same papers found in the focal area of the page. The bears' shirts were made by punching extra bears from red paper, then trimming off the unwanted areas. The faces and balloon strings were drawn with an acid-free pen.

Paper Pizazz™: *Vacation* (clouds)
Bear, balloon punches: Marvy® Uchida
Decorative scissors: cloud by Fiskars®, Inc.
Page designer: LeNae Gerig for Hot Off The Press, Inc.

Multi-layered mats are turned into lacy borders with a hole punch and decorative scissors. First cut the mat with decorative scissors, then punch between the scallops. The bunny punch is used to make a secondary border that ties into the photo and the die cut used for journaling.

Paper Pizazz™: *Romantic Papers*
Bunny die cut: Ellison® Craft & Design
Bunny punch: Marvy® Uchida
⅛" round punch: McGill, Inc.
Decorative scissors: scallop, cloud by Fiskars®, Inc.
Page designer: LeNae Gerig for Hot Off The Press, Inc.

© & ™ Ellison® Craft & Design

A brass stencil was used to emboss the package design around the border of this "gifted" page. Place the stencil on a flat, hard surface and position the paper to be embossed over it (this is easier if you place light behind the stencil, such as from a window or light box). Rub over the paper with a round stylus, pressing it firmly into the corners. The design will "pop" to the opposite side of the paper, so work on the back of the paper if it's important to have the raised area on the front.

Paper Pizazz™: *Christmas*
Brass gift stencil: Lasting Impressions
Decorative scissors: ripple by Fiskars®, Inc.
¼" round punch: McGill, Inc.
Page designer: LeNae Gerig for Hot Off The Press, Inc.

The same embossing technique described above was used here to create textured mats for these photos and text blocks plus the border on the background paper. After the border was embossed from the back of the background sheet, it was turned right side up and the stencil was replaced over the raised design. A cotton swab was used to lightly chalk the pattern.

Paper Pizazz™: *Country* (Irish chain quilt)
Brass corner, border stencils: American Traditional
Decorative scissors: deckle by Fiskars®, Inc.
Page designer: Anne-Marie Spencer for Hot Off The Press, Inc.

The simplest border of all: Use a pretty paper which coordinates with the theme and center a matted photo on it, leaving 1"–1½" of the paper visible all around.

Paper Pizazz™: *Holidays & Seasons* (embossed hearts)
Corner cutter: nostalgia by Fiskars®, Inc.
Page designer: Nancy Church for Pebbles in My Pocket

A 2" wide camouflage border is used to establish a sort-of-military theme for this page, echoed by trimming a photo in a camouflage shape and cutting others from solid paper to use as mats and accents.

Paper Pizazz™: *Great Outdoors* (camouflage)
Page designer: Allison Meyers for Memory Lane

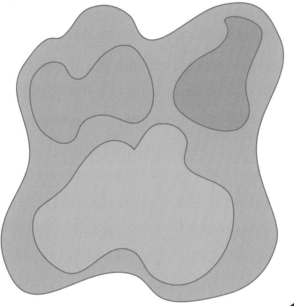

It's simple to add an artsy touch with a border like this—it's just ¾" strips of brown paper cut irregularly, with a few branches bumping out. Use a fine black pen to decorate it with knots and wood grain. A brown pen was used to decorate paper strips to form matching letters.

Paper Pizazz™: *Great Outdoors* (red/black plaid)
Page designer: Joy Huish for Pebbles in My Pocket

Patterned rulers make it easy to be an artist, allowing you to draw perfect pattern lines every time—almost essential to produce an effect like these wavy music staffs.

Paper Pizazz™: *Metallic Papers*
Wavy ruler: Déjà Views™ by C-Thru® Ruler Co.
Decorative scissors: scallop, mini scallop by Fiskars®, Inc.
Hexagon template: Extra Special Products
Rose, music note stickers: ©Mrs. Grossman's Paper Co.
Page designer: Debbie Peterson

A sumptuous tone-on-tone background is effective for these wedding photos. The ruler used to edge the background sheet is similar in appearance to the scissors used to edge the mats. Outlining it with gold creates an even more elegant look. The doilies are perfect for matting.

Paper Pizazz™: *Romantic Papers*
Decorative ruler: Déjà Views™ by C-Thru® Ruler Co.
Paper lace doilies: Artifacts, Inc.
Decorative scissors: colonial by Fiskars®, Inc.
Gold pen: Marvy® Uchida
Page designer: LeNae Gerig for Hot Off The Press, Inc.

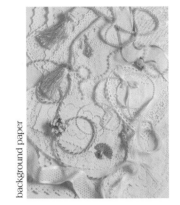

background paper

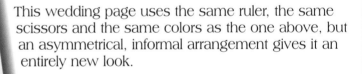

This wedding page uses the same ruler, the same scissors and the same colors as the one above, but an asymmetrical, informal arrangement gives it an entirely new look.

Paper Pizazz™: *Romantic Papers, Wedding* (white satin)
Decorative ruler: Déjà Views™ by C-Thru® Ruler Co.
Decorative scissors: colonial by Fiskars®, Inc.
Page designer: Katie Hacker for Hot Off The Press, Inc.

Rulers were used to make borders within borders for the top and bottom of this page. 2" strips were cut from both blue and violet solids. The edges of the violet strips were trimmed following the ruler pattern, then the violet strips were centered on the blue strips.

Paper Pizazz™: *Book of Firsts*
Decorative ruler: Déjà Views™ by C-Thru® Ruler Co.
Decorative scissors: ripple by Fiskars®, Inc.
1" heart punch: Marvy® Uchida
½" heart punch: Fiskars®, Inc.
Page designer: LeNae Gerig for Hot Off The Press, Inc.

An easy border appropriate for this page is composed of a 2" strip of the same bubble paper used to mat the photo, trimmed with a ⅝" strip of solid blue cut using a patterned ruler. Notice how creative journaling follows the ruler line.

Paper Pizazz™: *Baby* (bubbles), *Bright Great Backgrounds*
Decorative ruler: Déjà Views™ by C-Thru® Ruler Co.
Decorative scissors: seagull by Fiskars®, Inc.
Page designer: Becky Goughnour for Hot Off The Press, Inc.

Offset waves of blue made with a ruler increase the sense of motion in the centered waterfall paper.

Paper Pizazz™: *Great Outdoors* (water over rocks)
Wave ruler: Family Treasures
Decorative scissors: wave by Fiskars®, Inc.
Page designers: LeNae Gerig and Becky Goughnour for Hot Off The Press, Inc.

Reversing the ruler pattern to make waves in the blue papers creates an ocean lapping on a paper shore. The sky was done with layered freeform curves in sunset colors.

Paper Pizazz™: *Bright Great Backgrounds, Solid Muted Colors*
Decorative ruler: Déjà Views™ by C-Thru® Ruler Co.
Decorative scissors: deckle by Fiskars®, Inc.
Star, seashell punch: Marvy® Uchida
Alphabet stickers: Making Memories™
Silver pen: Marvy® Uchida
Page designer: LeNae Gerig for Hot Off The Press, Inc.

Bigger Pages

There are two camps of scrapbookers—those who prefer 8½"x11" pages and those who use 12"x12". This chapter features the work of designers who cleverly use the smaller sheets of Paper Pizazz™ to make larger album pages. How? By purposely placing the sheet to create areas for journaling, die cuts, stickers or other embellishments. The 8½"x11" papers can go in the centers of the 12"x12" album pages, along the bottoms, or offset in the middles for some wonderful looks (see pages 66–67).

The 8½"x11" sheets can be cut to form decorative borders (strips cut along the 11" side do a nice job of filling sides of a 12"x12" page; see the bottom of page 67). We couldn't resist showing a 12"x12" version of the matted wainscoting technique from the "Let's Split" chapter (see the bottom of page 72). Decorative corner treatments also allow 8½"x11" papers to effectively be used on larger album pages (see the tops of pages 72 and 68).

Designer Kathy Slack has found an innovative way to add reminiscences and family stories to her albums. See page 75 for Kathy's wonderful use of binders.

We're proud to say Paper Pizazz™ sheets are now available in the 12"x12" size—even Disney papers are in the larger size. However, we must confess the sheets are actually 11¾"x12" so they easily fit onto a 12"x12" page or slip into the new larger 12"x12" sheet protectors. Now we have everyone covered and there will be scrapbooks with pizazz everywhere!

**This chapter's background paper is from
Paper Pizazz™ Bright Great Backgrounds.**

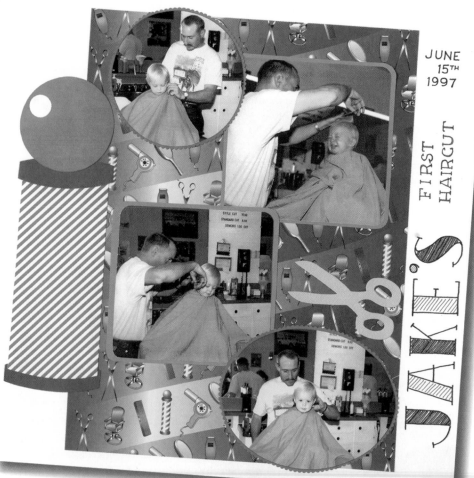

JUNE 15TH 1997

JAKE'S FIRST HAIRCUT

Centering an 8½"x11" patterned page on a scrapbook page could be boring, but allowing the photos and art to extend off the page adds visual interest. The wide margin is ideal for journaling. (The barber pole pattern is on page 142.)

Paper Pizazz™: *Christmas* (red & white stripe), *Book of Firsts*
Red, blue pens: Zig® by EK Success Ltd.
Scissors die cut: Ellison® Craft & Design
Decorative scissors: mini scallop by Fiskars®, Inc.
⅜" circle punch: Fiskars®, Inc.
Page designer: Becky Goughnour for Hot Off The Press, Inc.

© & ™ Ellison® Craft & Design

Place an 8½"x11" patterned page horizontally on the scrapbook space; leave a wide top border for a headline and embellishments.

Paper Pizazz™: *School Days* (crayons)
Bus, crayon cutouts: *Paper Pizazz™ School Days*
Red paint pen: Zig® by EK Success Ltd.
Decorative scissors: volcano by Fiskars®, Inc.
Page designer: LeNae Gerig for Hot Off The Press, Inc.

Offsetting an 8½"x11" patterned page helps to counterbalance the regular arrangement of oval photos. The action sequence, arranged around the center photo like the face of a clock, reinforces the idea of a fun and busy, but tiring day.

Paper Pizazz™: *Birthday* (party hats)
Stickers: Frances Meyer, Inc.®
Red, gold, green pens: EK Success, Ltd.
Decorative scissors: scallop by Fiskars®, Inc.
Page designer: LeNae Gerig for Hot Off The Press, Inc.

• punch eyes
• cut a leaf in half for wings
• trim star points for beak
• cut a snowflake in half for feet

THREE YEARS OLD

OCTOBER 1997

Scarecrow Alley

Cut strips lengthwise from an 8½"x11" patterned paper, then mount them horizontally on facing pages to draw the eye from one to the next. A decorative ruler was used to edge these strips for extra impact. The crows are assembled from punches—see above. (The scarecrow pattern is on page 138.)

Paper Pizazz™: *Holidays & Seasons* (candy corn)
Pumpkin stickers: Mary Engelbreit for Melissa Neufeld, Inc
Red, orange pens: Zig® by EK Success Ltd.
Decorative scissors: deckle by Fiskars®, Inc.

1" heart, 1" leaf, ½" snowflake punches: Family Treasures
Star, ⅛" and ½" circle punches: McGill, Inc.
Scarecrow die cut: Ellison® Craft & Design
Page designer: Stephanie Taylor

Borders and corners can expand the pattern area on a square page in an organized way. The 8½"x11" soccer-ball paper was trimmed into a square and centered on the page. 1½" solid red strips with ½" black strips in the centers form the borders. Matted circles cover the area where the strip ends don't quite meet.

Paper Pizazz™: *Sports* (soccer balls)
Soccer ball stickers: Frances Meyer, Inc.®
Corner Edger: art deco by Fiskars®, Inc.
Page designer: Stephanie Taylor

Cut three 3½" circles each from two or three patterned papers, then quarter them to make rounded triangles. Glue them as shown for a border with a braided look. (The apple and worm patterns are on page 142.)

Paper Pizazz™: *School Days* (yellow pad, crayons), *Ho Ho Ho* (Christmas plaid), *Country* (blue corrugated)
Apple, crayon, book, slate, ruler, star, alphabet stickers: Frances Meyer, Inc.®
Apple, worm, banner die cuts: Ellison® Craft & Design
Black, white paint pens: Zig® by EK Success Ltd.
Corner rounder: Fiskars®, Inc.
Page designer: Stephanie Taylor

What fun! A pen was used to draw Dalmatian spots all over the background page, which would boggle your eyes if not artfully broken up with borders and matted photos.

Paper Pizazz™: *Christmas* (red tartan)
Stickers: Stickopotamus™ by EK Success Ltd.
Metallic gold pen: Zig® by EK Success Ltd.
Page designer: Stephanie Taylor

A wave ruler was used to cut 2" wide strips from the long edges of the 8½"x11" patterned paper. The strips were then matted on solid green and mounted overlapping the edges of an 8½"x11" brown sheet, filling the 12"x12" page. The center sheet was decorated with hand-drawn trees to coordinate with the patterned paper, and a scene composed of die cuts was used to fill the page bottom, concealing the strip ends. (The bear and mountain patterns are on page 141.)

Paper Pizazz™: *Great Outdoors* (moose & deer)
Bear, mountains, pawprint die cuts: Ellison® Craft & Design
Ant stickers: ©Mrs. Grossman's Paper Co.
Gold, green pens: Zig® by EK Success Ltd.
Decorative ruler: Déjà Views™ by C-Thru® Ruler Co.
Decorative scissors: deckle by Fiskars®, Inc.
Page designer: Stephanie Taylor

Lay die-cut snowflakes on your 12"x12" page (repositionable adhesive helps hold them in place) and sponge over them, then remove the snowflakes. For a subtle color variation, three different blue markers were used directly on the face of the makeup sponge. Photo mats and letters die cut from 8½"x11" snowflake-patterned paper complete the effect.

Paper Pizazz™: *Christmas* (snowflakes)
Snowflake, alphabet die cuts: Ellison® Craft & Design
Colored markers: Marvy® Uchida
Page designer: Stephanie Taylor

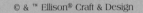

© & ™ Ellison® Craft & Design

You don't have to be an artist to create a lush background like this. The large leaves were die cut; the vines, grass and critters are all stickers. Note how the stickers overlap and extend under the photos to pull them right into the wilderness. (The palm leaf patterns are on page 140.)

Paper Pizazz™: *Pets* (grass)
Jungle leaf die cuts: Ellison® Craft & Design
Leaf, vine, grass, critter stickers: ©Mrs. Grossman's Paper Co.
Green pens: Zig® by EK Success Ltd.
Page designer: Stephanie Taylor

You get a lot of effect from a small investment when you use 8½"x11" patterned papers for large die-cut letters, then arrange them to border the page like this. Cropping the photos in circles and suspending them as ornaments ties in with the Christmas theme.

Paper Pizazz™: *Christmas* (holly)
Flower, bow punches: Family Treasures
Alphabet die cuts: Ellison® Craft & Design
Gold pen: Marvy® Uchida
Page designer: Allison Meyers for Memory Lane

2" circles cut with a template frame punched trees, forming a border for this portrait page. The brightness of the 8½"x11" patterned background paper pops the photo forward.

Paper Pizazz™: *Ho Ho Ho* (ho ho ho)
Tree punch: Marvy® Uchida
Decorative scissors: deckle by Fiskars®, Inc.
Page designer: Stephanie Taylor

These fancy corners are built up of four paper layers, then topped with real lace for a special, romantic feeling. The 8½"x11" rose paper is centered on the larger album page. Remember to copy any newspaper article onto acid-free, lignin-free paper and use the copy in your album (newsprint contains acid and lignin).

Paper Pizazz™: *Romantic Papers*
Lace: Venus Decorative Ribbon
Calligraphy pen: Pigma Callipen by Sakura
Decorative scissors: colonial by Fiskars®, Inc.
Page designer: Katie Hacker for Hot Off The Press, Inc.

Divide the 8½"x11" patterned paper into four equal lengthwise strips, then mat each separately. Mount them horizontally on a 12"x12" page to create an overall look of richness. The paper lace was matted on a solid pink paper to keep the intricate design viewable.

Paper Pizazz™: *Metallic Papers, Pretty Papers* (cream roses)
Laser-cut lace: *Paper Pizazz™ Romantic Papers*
Round punch: Fiskars®, Inc.
Calligraphy pen: Pigma Callipen by Sakura
Page designer: Becky Goughnour for Hot Off The Press, Inc.

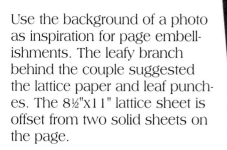

Use the background of a photo as inspiration for page embellishments. The leafy branch behind the couple suggested the lattice paper and leaf punches. The 8½"x11" lattice sheet is offset from two solid sheets on the page.

Paper Pizazz™: *Wedding* (lattice)
Leaf punch: Family Treasures
Embossed frame: Making Memories™
Page designer: Kathy Slack

Like the page above, this one uses an 8½"x11" patterned paper offset on a solid to create an asymmetrical border. Edged diagonal strips of the same solid fill the right edge of the page, framing the journaling.

Paper Pizazz™: *Wedding*
Leaf die cuts: Ellison® Craft & Design
Corner edger: nostalgia by Fiskars®, Inc.
Page designer: Kathy Slack

© & ™ Ellison® Craft & Design

Cutting an 8½"x11" leaf-patterned paper diagonally from corner to corner provides two large corners and leaves a plain background for display of the photo and text. A 3" background strip and extra leaves cut from another sheet of the same paper draw your eye inward.

Paper Pizazz™: *Great Outdoors* (frosted leaves), *Solid Muted Colors*
Page designer: Kathy Slack

Meryl Slack
May 10, 1918 ~ August 30 1941
J. B. Montgomery Trucking Co.
Wages $46.00 per week
One of many, who gave his life to the
Profession of Trucking!
With sacrifice of Family and Friends.

Their small size means keepsakes such as this wedding folder are often lost or damaged. Mounting the folder on an album page with a wedding photo protects both for future generations to enjoy.

Paper Pizazz™: *Great Outdoors* (water over rocks), *Pretty Papers* (green marble)
Page designer: Kathy Slack

Record
Of Our
Wedding

Storybook Pages

A family history, stories and memories compiled from older members of your family, a collection of letters from a son or daughter away at college or in the military—often you have more information and explanation to support your photos than will fit in a few lines of journaling. Creating a "book page" allows you to use as many story pages as you require, and makes a priceless legacy for future generations. Such a page makes a good starting page for an album of historic photos.

Use a 3-prong binder with a clear cover. Glue it to the left side of your 12"x12" album page, or attach it with cord and secure with double-stick tape. Decorate the title page to coordinate with the album page. Extra pages can be added at any time.

The Slack Story is a compilation of five generations of family history. Each generation's history and statistics were printed on a different solid Paper Pizazz™ color. The photos were framed with cutouts from *Black & White Photos*, reduced in size on a color copier to fit along the right edge of the page.

It's important to gather information and stories from as many sources as possible. Some stories may conflict with others; that's okay. Include both sides and let your readers draw their own conclusions as they enjoy getting to know previous generations and learning about their heritage.

Paper Pizazz™: *Wedding, Black & White Photos*
Border tape: Chartpak®
Page designer: Kathy Slack

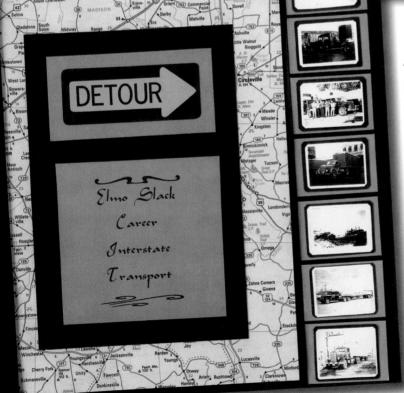

The same format was used for this history of Elmo Slack's career in interstate transport. In addition to pertinent personal information and reminiscences, the text includes important items of historical interest such as wages, cost per mile at different times, and his exemption from World War II military service because he was hauling bomb parts.

Paper Pizazz™: *Vacation* (road map)
Detour cutout: *Paper Pizazz™ Vacation*
Page designer: Kathy Slack

Hi Mom!
I took this
photo because it
looks so English
Lincoln county
seat for Lincoln-
shire home of
Robin Hood
Love Katie

Miss you, Laura!
The beautiful
Lake District
inspired the
Romantic Poets
Beatrix Potter
lived there, too.
Be good!
Your Sis ~ Katie

Dear Craig,
The South Downs,
an old mountain
range — some of
the prettiest
countryside in
England These sheep
are along The Roman
Road See you soon —
Katie

FUNNY
FACES
of JOSEPH
9-15-97

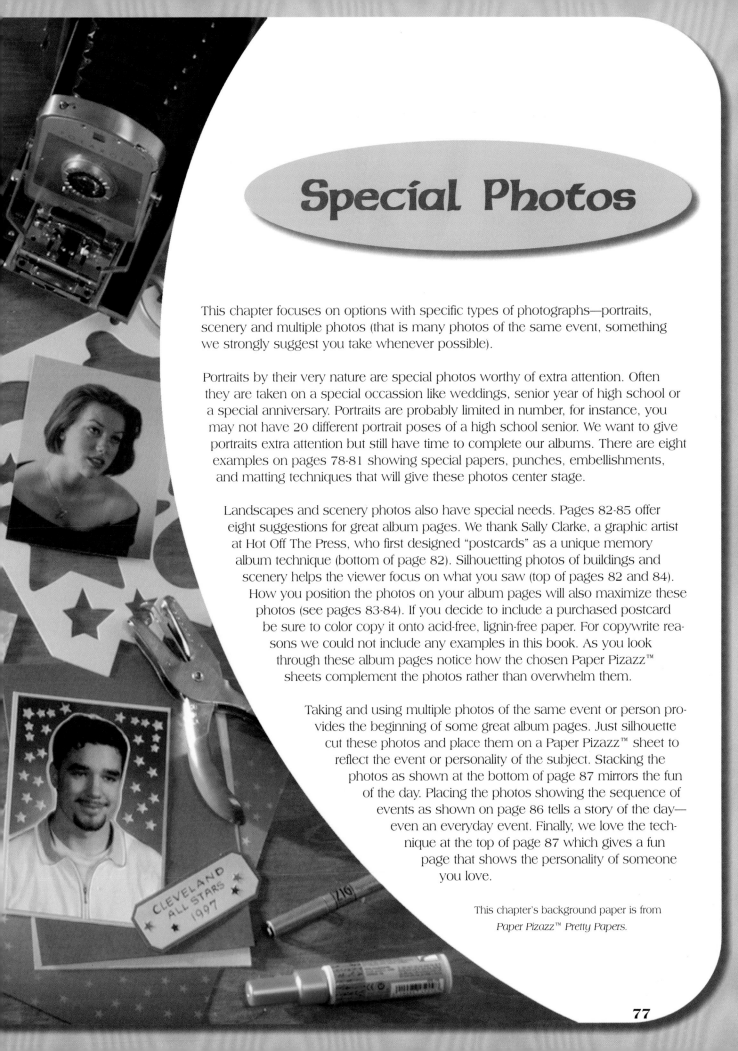

Special Photos

This chapter focuses on options with specific types of photographs—portraits, scenery and multiple photos (that is many photos of the same event, something we strongly suggest you take whenever possible).

Portraits by their very nature are special photos worthy of extra attention. Often they are taken on a special occassion like weddings, senior year of high school or a special anniversary. Portraits are probably limited in number, for instance, you may not have 20 different portrait poses of a high school senior. We want to give portraits extra attention but still have time to complete our albums. There are eight examples on pages 78-81 showing special papers, punches, embellishments, and matting techniques that will give these photos center stage.

Landscapes and scenery photos also have special needs. Pages 82-85 offer eight suggestions for great album pages. We thank Sally Clarke, a graphic artist at Hot Off The Press, who first designed "postcards" as a unique memory album technique (bottom of page 82). Silhouetting photos of buildings and scenery helps the viewer focus on what you saw (top of pages 82 and 84). How you position the photos on your album pages will also maximize these photos (see pages 83-84). If you decide to include a purchased postcard be sure to color copy it onto acid-free, lignin-free paper. For copywrite reasons we could not include any examples in this book. As you look through these album pages notice how the chosen Paper Pizazz™ sheets complement the photos rather than overwhelm them.

Taking and using multiple photos of the same event or person provides the beginning of some great album pages. Just silhouette cut these photos and place them on a Paper Pizazz™ sheet to reflect the event or personality of the subject. Stacking the photos as shown at the bottom of page 87 mirrors the fun of the day. Placing the photos showing the sequence of events as shown on page 86 tells a story of the day— even an everyday event. Finally, we love the technique at the top of page 87 which gives a fun page that shows the personality of someone you love.

This chapter's background paper is from
Paper Pizazz™ Pretty Papers.

Portraits

Give a very special look to holiday portraits with glittering metallics and special "double double" mats. First these photos were matted on black, then the corners were trimmed. The black mats were mounted on silver paper trimmed ⅛" away to leave narrow contoured outlines. Each double-matted photo was then double-matted again on the same two colors, this time with a simple rectangular mat.

Paper Pizazz™: *Metallic Papers*
Silver paper: Hygloss Products, Inc.
Corner cutter: celestial by Fiskars®, Inc.
Tree die cut: Ellison® Craft & Design
Silver pen: Marvy® Uchida
Page designer: LeNae Gerig and
    Becky Goughnour for Hot Off
    The Press, Inc.

Border punches add a designer touch when they're used like this on an offset mat, then lined with a gold paper. Note that the black mat surrounds both photos continuously, but is offset and punched on the opposite corner of each. Add this page to your list of corner techniques.

Paper Pizazz™: *Pretty Papers* (tapestry),
    Metallic Papers
Border punch: McGill, Inc.
Gold pens: Marvy® Uchida
Page designer: Becky Goughnour for Hot
    Off The Press, Inc.

All by themselves, layered mats of rich-looking papers create an opulent effect. When different edge treatments are used the textural differences add interest. Narrow outlines drawn with a silver pen give this romantic page extra punch.

Paper Pizazz™: *Wedding* (white satin), *Pretty Papers* (blue swirl), *Bright Great Backgrounds*

Pansy cutouts: *Romantic Papers*

Decorative scissors: colonial by Fiskars®, Inc.

Corner rounder: Family Treasures

Silver pen: Marvy® Uchida

Page designer: Katie Hacker for Hot Off The Press, Inc.

Multiple mats can be very subtle. This stunning portrait is quadruple-matted on three shades of paper, but the narrow edges simply add depth. The curved edges of two laser-cut lace border sheets are turned inward to focus your eye on the beauty of the bride.

Paper Pizazz™: *Wedding* (pink moiré)

Laser-cut lace: *Paper Pizazz™ Romantic Papers*

Decorative scissors: mini Victorian by Family Treasures

Page designer: LeNae Gerig for Hot Off The Press, Inc.

In contrast to the album pages shown on page 79, this page is pure fun, with its brightly patterned papers and mixture of designs. The diagonal mat keeps the page balanced, but helps it avoid too much symmetry.

Paper Pizazz™: *Birthday)* (colorful stripes), *School Days* (colorful dots—the school equipment sheet is not sold separately)
Decorative scissors: zipper by Fiskars®, Inc.
Heart punch: Marvy® Uchida
Page designer: LeNae Gerig for Hot Off The Press, Inc.

© & ™ Ellison® Craft & Design

Here's a great example of making die cuts from both patterned and plain papers. Die-cut chickie pins and overlapped hearts add a whimsical touch to a sweet baby portrait. Note that the oval photo is placed on a triple rectangular mat, with the center mat edged to match the portrait.

Paper Pizazz™: *Pretty Papers* (purple sponged), *Light Great Backgrounds*
Decorative scissors: seagull, stamp by Fiskars®, Inc.
Diaper pin, heart die cuts: Ellison® Craft & Design
Blue pen: Marvy® Uchida
Page designer: Anne-Marie Spencer for Hot Off The Press, Inc.

Black and white photos look best on more traditional papers such as this old-fashioned Christmas collage. The mat colors were matched to the background for a coordinated look. The punched lace technique used for the mats of the focal photo is in keeping with the vintage effect, and it's so easy to do—just cut a wide mat with decorative scissors and punch holes.

Paper Pizazz™: *Romantic Papers*
Decorative scissors: seagull by Fiskars®, Inc.
⅛" round punch:
    McGill, Inc.
Page designer: LeNae
    Gerig for Hot Off
    The Press, Inc.

It's a boy! A wide mat is used to list his vital statistics, and the drummer bear is marching off to spread the news.

Paper Pizazz™: *Baby* (It's a Boy)
Bear cutout: *Paper Pizazz™ Little Charmers*
Gold pen: Marvy® Uchida
Page designer: LeNae Gerig for Hot Off
    The Press, Inc.

Scenery

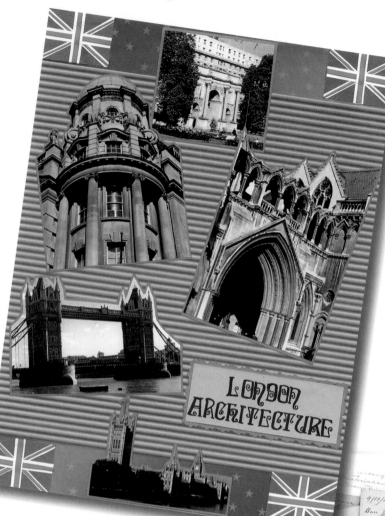

All these photos of buildings could be confusing, but varying the sizes and silhouetting some, then setting them at different angles keeps your eye moving. The British flags not only identify the locale, but also corral your eye and keep the focus inside the page.

Paper Pizazz™: *Country* (blue corrugated), *Adult Birthday* (blue stars)
Decorative scissors: ripple by Fiskars®, Inc.
Page designer: Anne-Marie Spencer for Hot Off The Press, Inc.

3"x6" postcards are a natural for scenery photos, especially when you want to journal them more completely. Hand-drawn postmarks date the photos, while the punched "stamps" remind us that however far we travel, home is where the heart is. Notice each postcard has a 2-sided mat.

Paper Pizazz™: *Black & White Photos* (letters)
Decorative scissors: deckle by Fiskars®, Inc.
Heart punch: Fiskars®, Inc.
Page designer: LeNae Gerig for Hot Off The Press, Inc.

The focal photo doesn't necessarily have to be the largest one on the page. The eye naturally goes to the human face or figure, and this little girl's placement in the center of the page also helps make her the focus. Trimming the corners of the scenic pictures to follow the oval shape of the center photo reinforces the idea that she's most important.

Paper Pizazz™: *Great Outdoors* (ferns)
Decorative scissors: deckle by Fiskars®, Inc.
Gold pen: Marvy® Uchida
Page designer: LeNae Gerig for Hot Off The Press, Inc.

Use a panoramic camera to photograph an expansive view, then comment on it with inset photos taken from different angles.

Paper Pizazz™: *Vacation* (shells)
Decorative scissors: wave by Fiskars®, Inc.
Page designer: LeNae Gerig for Hot Off The Press, Inc.

Photos taken at different distances, enlarged and cropped with irregular top lines, create a downward-flowing movement that is appropriate for the waterfall photos. This technique gives an expansive view of the scenery while still allowing the closeup of the family to be the focus of the page.

Paper Pizazz™: *Vacation*
Decorative scissors: deckle by Fiskars®, Inc.
Page designer: Becky Goughnour for Hot Off The Press, Inc.

Frame views of distant scenery with closer items, such as the fence and tree branches in the central photo, to provide a sense of perspective.

Paper Pizazz™: *Pretty Papers* (green marble)
Decorative scissors: mini Victorian by Family Treasures
Page designer: Becky Goughnour for Hot Off The Press, Inc.

Many scenery photos, especially close-ups such as this flower garden, have an overall pattern with no clear focus. It is effective to split these photos up as page accents. Here the capital letters were cut from the lower corner of the photo (these were cut freehand, but you could also die cut them). The rest of the photo was used as a wide off-set mat for the town square shot.

Paper Pizazz™: *Pretty Papers* (purple sponged)

5.0 calligraphy pen: Zig® by EK Success Ltd.

Page designer: LeNae Gerig for Hot Off The Press, Inc.

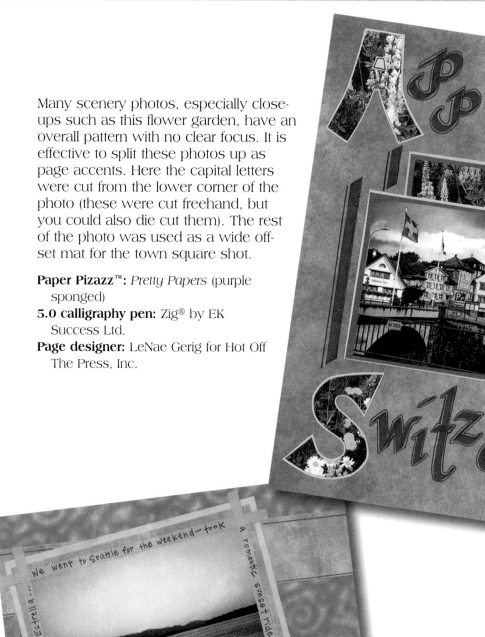

Bright patterns CAN work for scenery. The coral, gold and violets used on this page reflect the colors of the sunset and the neon of the marketplace. The ¼" wide border strips are handy for journaling.

Paper Pizazz™: *Bright Great Backgrounds*

Page designer: Katie Hacker for Hot Off The Press, Inc.

Multiple Photos

A sequence of photographs used together like this anchor an event in time and produce the feeling of freeze-frame action. The narrow, bright mats separate the photos, while overlapping them keeps the sense of action.

Paper Pizazz™: *Birthday* (candles)
Numeral cutouts: *Paper Pizazz™ Adult Birthday*
Decorative scissors: mini pinking by Fiskars®, Inc.
Page designer: LeNae Gerig for Hot Off The Press, Inc.

A series of action photos can be arranged on a page to create a fluid sense of motion. The slight overlap of these photos of Zakkery draws the viewer's eye through an entire morning of play. Journaling around the silhouettes accentuates the feeling of movement.

Paper Pizazz™: *Adult Birthday* (blue stars)
Decorative scissors: volcano by Fiskars®, Inc.
Red pen: Zig® by EK Success Ltd.
¼", ½" star punches: Family Treasures
Wagon stickers: ©Mrs. Grossman's Paper Co.
Page designer: LeNae Gerig for Hot Off The Press, Inc.

Overlapped multiple shots of the same person provide a photographic character study. To prevent photos with similar colors from running together, outline mat them in bright colors.

Paper Pizazz™: *Bright Great Backgrounds*
Decorative scissors: dragonback by Fiskars®, Inc.
Page designer: LeNae Gerig for Hot Off The Press, Inc.

Overlapping two rows or more rows of people produces a three-dimensional look, and also avoids the awkward cut-off-at-the-waist appearance many closeup photos have.

Paper Pizazz™: *Birthday* (confetti)
Mortarboard cutouts: *Paper Pizazz™ School Days*
Decorative scissors: ripple by Fiskars®, Inc.
Page designer: Katie Hacker for Hot Off The Press, Inc.

WOW! Pages

Some album pages just wouldn't fit into a category, so we offer them to you here. Using quilting patterns is a tried and true method of making wonderful album pages. There are ten album page examples on pages 90–94. They use several quilt patterns including a simple patchwork, Grandmother's Fan and Log Cabin. Since quilting primarily uses geometric shapes, they work well when made out of Paper Pizazz™.

We must thank the magazine *Memory Makers*, where we first saw album pages based on stained glass designs. We credit Narda Poe from Texas for developing this technique. Although this method is a bit time-consuming, these album pages are not hard to do and the results are wonderful, as you'll see on page 95.

Susan Shea is a graphic designer at Hot Off The Press. She applied her training in using Paper Pizazz™ to make collages based on photographs. Her technique requires only three black & white photocopies of the photograph and sheets of Paper Pizazz™. What fantastic results on pages 96–97! Thank you, Susan.

The final pages of this chapter feature four album pages we love. The tie dye on page 99 is an example of a "Why didn't I think of that?" page. Cutting a tie-dye sheet of Paper Pizazz™ into a t-shirt seems so obvious––that is, after you see it. Likewise using the two sheets of laser-cut lace from the *Paper Pizazz™ Romantic Papers* book, cutting them and placing the straight edges around a portrait gives a wonderful look, easily (see the top of page 98).

This chapter's background paper is from
Paper Pizazz™ Light Great Backgrounds.

2⅝" square quilt blocks are an excellent way to display several views of the same subject. Templates make it easy to cut matching squares and hearts. Drawn black lines and dots simulate stitching.

Paper Pizazz™: *Romantic Papers, Light Great Backgrounds*
Heart template: Extra Special Products, Inc.
White paint pen: Zig® by EK Success Ltd.
Decorative scissors: mini scallop by Fiskars®, Inc.
Page designer: Becky Goughnour for Hot Off The Press, Inc.

A more elaborate quilt design uses a large center photo surrounded by two patchwork borders, each created with stickers and punches. The Xs are ¼"x1¼" strips, decorated with stitches and crossed. The cherries were made with a ½" circle punch, the leaves with a ½" heart punch. Paint pens were used to draw a white highlight and a brown stem on each cherry.

Paper Pizazz™: *Christmas* (white dot on green)
Stickers: Mary Engelbreit for Melissa Neufeld, Inc.
¼" circle punch: McGill, Inc.
Heart, ½" circle punches: Fiskars®, Inc.
White, brown paint pens: Zig® by EK Success, Ltd.
Page designer: LeNae Gerig for Hot Off The Press, Inc.

A traditional quilt pattern interpreted in different papers makes a good background. Using a die to cut the shapes ensures that they match exactly. This pastel Grandmother's Fan quilt is especially nice with the quilt background of the photos.

Paper Pizazz™: *Baby* (pastel hearts, pastel stripes, pastel dots, pastel quilt)
Foot stickers: Frances Meyer, Inc.®
Decorative scissors: scallop, mini scallop by Fiskars®, Inc.
Fan die cut: Ellison® Craft & Design
Page designer: LeNae Gerig for Hot Off The Press, Inc.

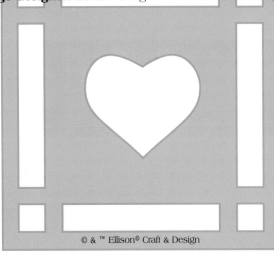

Use both the positive and negative cut shapes from six quilt blocks to make a mix-and-match album quilt. Each block was die cut from a different paper, then the hearts, squares and strips from one block were glued into the matching holes of another. Extra shapes were cut to embellish the borders.

Paper Pizazz™: *Light Great Backgrounds*
Quilt block die cut: Ellison® Craft & Design
Decorative scissors: scallop by Fiskars®, Inc.
Page designer: LeNae Gerig for Hot Off The Press, Inc.

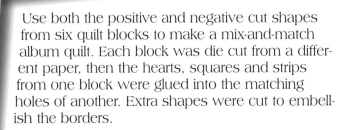

1" squares of swirl paper were cut diagonally to make the triangles which surround this square photo. A 1" strip of the same paper below the triangles turns the design area into a rectangle, leaving 1" top and bottom borders. The triangles are echoed in the journaling block.

Paper Pizazz™: *Black & White Photos* (brown & gold swirl, crushed suede)
Gold pens: Marvy® Uchida
Page designer: LeNae Gerig for Hot Off The Press, Inc.

Drawing its inspiration from the background paper, this country-look page is bordered by 1" blue strips "quilted" with paper triangles and drawn stitches. Besides reinforcing the theme, the sewing cutouts help to balance the page.

Paper Pizazz™: *Country* (country dots, sewing)
Spool, star, heart cutouts: *Paper Pizazz™ Country*
Decorative scissors: pinking by Fiskars®, Inc.
Page designer: LeNae Gerig for Hot Off The Press, Inc.

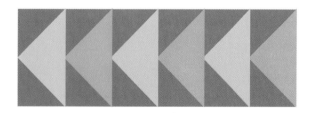

from *Romantic Papers*

purple sponged

lavender swirl

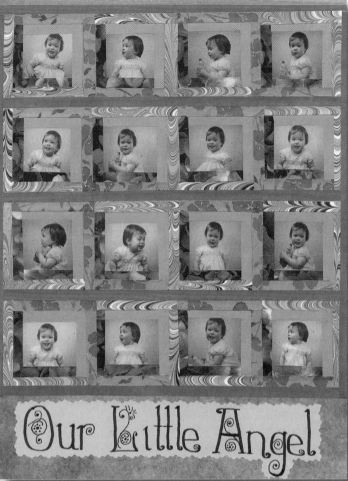

Cut ¼" strips of coordinated papers to build Log Cabin squares around small photos. Note that despite the apparently random swirl of colors, only three paper colors were used for each block, and there are only two arrangements.

Paper Pizazz™: *Romantic Papers, Pretty Papers* (purple sponged, lavender swirl)

Decorative scissors: ripple by Fiskars®, Inc.
Page designer: Anne-Marie Spencer for Hot Off The Press, Inc.

The simplest quilt pattern to sew is a series of borders around a large center panel. Applied to photos and papers, the same technique makes a ten-minute album page that's as spectacular as it is easy. Paper stars decorated with stitches resemble appliqué, but take much less time!

Paper Pizazz™: *Ho Ho Ho* (white dot on red, red & green dots, Christmas plaid, green plaid) *Christmas* (red & green stripe, white dot on green, red tartan), *Vacation* (pine trees)
2" star template: Provo Craft®
1" star punch: Marvy® Uchida
Page designer: Becky Goughnour for Hot Off The Press, Inc.

93

¾" strips of coordinating pastel prints were woven together to make the patchwork background for this page. To make construction easier and keep your weaving straight, draw a grid on a plain background sheet and tack the ends of the strips down with repositionable glue.

Paper Pizazz™: *Baby* (pastel dots, pastel hearts, pastel stripes)
Decorative scissors: ripple by Fiskars®, Inc.
Page designer: Anne-Marie Spencer for Hot Off The Press, Inc.

Soft colors are a good choice for black and white photos. This page, built almost entirely from rectangles and triangles of three papers, is softened by the punched hearts. Setting the photo at an angle pops it forward. The "stitching" lines were drawn on.

Paper Pizazz™: *Light Great Backgrounds*
Heart punch: Marvy® Uchida
Page designer: LeNae Gerig for Hot Off The Press, Inc.

Stained Glass Look:

A step beyond quilt squares, this technique involves tracing a design onto a photo (or photocopy) and cutting the photo along the design lines. The photo is then reassembled like a jigsaw puzzle on a solid background, leaving uniform ⅛"–¼" gaps between the pieces.

Replace some of the outer pieces with patterned paper pieces to add interest to the border. On this page the three oval inner rows are all photo pieces, the outer rectangle row is all paper and the inner rectangle is a combination. The assembled photo was mounted on solid blue, then matted on outdoorsy patterned paper.

Paper Pizazz™: *Great Outdoors* (paddling), *Bright Great Backgrounds*

Page designer: Anne-Marie Spencer for Hot Off The Press, Inc.

A classic rose window was the inspiration for this page, which uses curved lines and a dramatic black background. These corner designs were cut with an X-acto® knife, but a corner punch could also be used.

Paper Pizazz™: *Black & White Photos* (brown & gold swirl, crushed suede)

Page designer: Anne-Marie Spencer for Hot Off The Press, Inc.

95

A

Paper Pizazz™ Portraits:

Definitely NOT 5-minute pages, but well worth the effort when you want an extra special portrait. It's not as hard as it looks; just follow the steps.

1 Select a photo with a clear image having obvious contrast and one strong light source originating from the top or side. (Direct frontal lighting such as flash photos, back lighting, or multiple light sources flatten the image, making it difficult to work with.)

2 Make three black-and-white photocopies of your photo, sizing them up or down as needed. The photocopies make it easy to determine the light and dark values in the photos. Choose papers (you'll need at least three) to reflect the different values. For a realistic effect, choose papers that are design-appropriate like the wood paper for a fence.

3 Transfer each value area to a sheet of Paper Pizazz™. Place wax-free transfer paper right side down on the patterned paper, then place a photocopy over it. Use a stylus or sharp pencil to trace the areas of that value. You may need to extend some background areas to fit your page, as was done with the meadow area for this page. Remove the photocopy and transfer paper, then cut out the pieces. Repeat for each value area.

4 Cut out the image from one photocopy. (**A**) Position it on a piece of plain paper as you will want it on your album page and glue it down. (**B**) Working from the largest background piece forward, glue the pieces over the corresponding areas of the photocopy—use repositionable adhesive. (**C**) Attach the foreground value shapes. Cut the portrait from the photocopy. Straighten and rearrange pieces if necessary.

5 Select a background paper for your page and glue the paper portrait to it. Using your third photocopy for reference, place the smallest detail shapes. Erase any transfer marks, then complete the page as desired with photos and journaling.

B

C

Paper Pizazz™: *Adult Birthday* (blue stars), *Country* (barnwood), *Pets* (grass), *Baby* (pastel dots), *Black & White Photos* (black & white swirl), *Pretty Papers* (green marble), *Romantic Papers, Light Great Backgrounds*
Silver pen: Marvy® Uchida
White paint pen: Zig® by EK Success Ltd.
Frame template: Déjà Views™ by C-Thru® Ruler Co.
Page designer: Susan Shea for Hot Off The Press, Inc.

A lighthouse Paper Pizazz™ portrait against a cloudy sky goes well with these beach photos. Notice how the fence crosses in front of one photo to provide a sense of perspective.

Paper Pizazz™: *Vacation* (clouds), *Country* (denim), *Wedding* (white moiré), *Black & White Photos* (black & white swirl), *Bright Great Backgrounds*
Frame template: Déjà Views™ by C-Thru® Ruler Co.
Page designer: Susan Shea for Hot Off The Press, Inc.

Unlike the previous two pages, in which the portrait was a background and commentary on the photos, the two portraits below were designed to stand alone. Note that choosing natural colors produces a fairly realistic portrait of the dog, while using shades of blue in the lower portrait creates an abstract, rather dreamy effect for John Denver.

Paper Pizazz™: *Black & White Photos* (brown & gold swirl, crushed suede), *Great Outdoors* (brown plaid, campfire), *Pretty Papers, Light Great Backgrounds, Bright Great Backgrounds, Solid Muted Colors*
Page designer: Susan Shea for Hot Off The Press, Inc.

Paper Pizazz™: *Adult Birthday* (blue stars), *Vacation* (clouds), *Wedding* (white moiré), *Bright Great Backgrounds*
Page designer: Susan Shea for Hot Off The Press, Inc.

 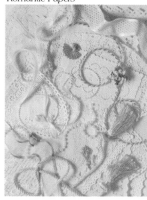

Heritage photos deserve special treatment. Romantic-looking papers set off with gold mats make page borders and fancy frames which enrich without overwhelming. For contrast against the golds and ivories of the background, the names were first written in black, then traced with the gold pen, leaving a narrow black border.

Paper Pizazz™: *Romantic Papers, Metallic Papers*
Laser-cut lace: *Paper Pizazz™ Romantic Papers*
Black, gold paint pens: Marvy® Uchida
Decorative scissors: Victorian by Fiskars®, Inc.
Page designer: Anne-Marie Spencer for Hot Off The Press, Inc.

Beautiful frames can be made from plain paper by tracing a stencil. Use small, sharp scissors or an X-acto® knife to cut out the traced shape; trim the photo to fit in the opening.

Paper Pizazz™: *Black & White Photos* (crushed suede)
Heart, plaque stencils: American Traditional
Decorative scissors: Victorian by Fiskars®, Inc.
Page designer: Anne-Marie Spencer for Hot Off The Press, Inc.

Everything about this page tells a story: The tie-dyed shirt in the background, the sequence of action in the photos and the wrap-around journaling. (The t-shirt pattern is on page 140.)

Paper Pizazz™: *Teen Years* (tie dye)
Red paint pen: Zig® by EK Success Ltd.
Gold paint pen: Marvy® Uchida
Decorative scissors: deckle by Fiskars®, Inc.
Page designer: Becky Goughnour for Hot Off The Press, Inc.

When there's no obvious theme uniting the photos you want to use, create one! The brightly colored 1"–2" gumballs filling this machine make "instant wow!"

Paper Pizazz™: *Birthday* (colorful stripes)
White paint pen: Zig by EK Success Ltd.
Circle template: Extra Special Products
Page designer: Katie Hacker for Hot Off The Press, Inc.

Lettering with Becky

Sometimes you find just what you need right next door. That's what happened when we needed an experienced scrapbooker and calligrapher. Becky Goughnour lives just down the street. Since she joined our team, she has been placed in a room filled with papers, punches, templates, and all manner of scrapbooking supplies. She seems quite happy and we're delighted with her results.

Becky wants to make journaling easier and less intimidating for others. In this chapter she shares 13 lettering styles, beginning with the easiest, which is stick lettering. Becky offers three variations of this simple style, embellishing the letters with balls, hearts or stars (sometimes she puts punched-out stars on the letters, too).

Some of Becky's lettering is done on directly on patterned Paper Pizazz™, which offers yet another look. On page 105 a bubble lettering style is shown on plain paper and on a sheet of bubbles for a terrific look. A plain lettering style is offered on page 106 which is shown with punches for embellishment and, another option, with two Paper Pizazz™ papers—a great look! On page 107 there is a lettering style which also can be done on patterned paper. This one has broken lines inside each letter for a quilted look. Another style, on page 111, also offers room to use a patterned paper which coordinates with the theme of the page. Any small patterned paper is a great background for these lettering styles.

The secret to great lettering? Becky says confidence plays an important part. "Just relax and don't worry about making perfect lettering," offers Becky. "In the beginning do special lettering only for the titles of your most important pages. As with any new skill, use the easiest lettering styles at first and move on as you feel comfortable. Also don't be afraid of using your own handwriting. The more you do it, the more confidence you'll have."

This chapter's background paper is from *Paper Pizazz™ Light Great Backgrounds*.

Stick Alphabets

Basic "stick printing" is a clean, simple, versatile style which can be adapted to anyone's own handwriting. It can be varied with different ink colors, sizes or line widths, by cutting out and matting it as shown at right, or by embellishing it with dots, hearts, stars or other figures chosen to suit the theme of your page.

Matthew's name was outlined in red, then matted on black to match the double-matted photo and die cut. It was turned to run along the edge of the page to fill an otherwise empty area.

Paper Pizazz™: *Sports* (soccer balls), *Pets* (grass)
Soccer ball die cut: Ellison® Craft & Design
Red paint pen: Zig® by EK Success Ltd.
Page designer: Becky Goughnour for Hot Off The Press, Inc.

ABCDEFGHIJKLMNOP
QRSTUVWXYZ abcdef
ghijklmnopqrstuvwxyz
1234567890

dots
ABCDEFGHIJKLMNOPQRSTUVWXYZ
abcdefghijklmnopqrstuvwxyz0123456789

hearts
abcdefghijklmnopqrstuvwxyz0123456789

stars
abcdefghijklmnopqrstuvwxyz0123456789

102

Not all the text on a page has to be the same. The headline on this page was done with a broad paint pen, decorated with hearts and outlined in black. The journaling on the flower is simpler, smaller ball-and-stick letters. The photos were shadowed to pop them forward. The rose was cut once from red and once from green paper, then the die cuts were trimmed and aligned to form a complete two-color rose.

Paper Pizazz™: *Ho Ho Ho* (white dot on red), *Metallic Papers*
Rose die cut: Ellison® Craft & Design
White paint pen: Zig® by EK Success Ltd.
Page designer: Becky Goughnour for Hot Off The Press, Inc.

© & ™ Ellison®
Craft & Design

An easy way to embellish stick letters is with small punches or stickers which contribute to the theme. Here the stars were punched and glued to the white letters, then each letter was outlined in silver for extra punch. (The heart pattern is on page 138.)

Paper Pizazz™: *Ho Ho Ho* (red & white stripes), *Light Great Backgrounds*
Star punch: Family Treasures
White paint pen: Zig® by EK Success, Ltd.
Silver pen: Marvy® Uchida
Decorative scissors: deckle, seagull by Fiskars®, Inc.
Page designer: Becky Goughnour for Hot Off The Press, Inc.

Outline Letters

are one step beyond stick printing. Start with simple stick letters drawn lightly in pencil, then outline them. Erase the pencil lines or paint over them. To cut out the letters, first draw them on plain paper or tracing paper, then trace or transfer them onto the patterned paper.

Use offset mats to create spaces for journaling on a tight page. These captioned photos will have so much meaning when Christopher is 21! The headline was filled in with red and decorated with curlicues and dots to match the festive mood.

Paper Pizazz™: *Light Great Backgrounds*
Cupcakes: *Paper Pizazz™ Celebration Punch-Outs™*
Decorative scissors: scallop from Fiskars®, Inc.
Red paint pen: Zig® by EK Success Ltd.
Page designer: Becky Goughnour for Hot Off The Press, Inc.

ABCDEF
GHIJKLMNOP
QRSTUVWXYZ
abcdefghijklm
nopqrstuvwxy
z 1234567890

Curving the lines outward makes letters which resemble clouds or bubbles, especially appropriate for outdoor or water-related photos. Not only the lettering, but the background paper and everything else on this page contribute to the fishbowl look. (The fishbowl pattern is on page 139.)

Paper Pizazz™: *Childhood* (big bubbles)
Bubble, fish stickers: Frances Meyer, Inc.®
Page designer: LeNae Gerig and Becky Goughnour for Hot Off The Press, Inc.

ABCDEFGHIJKLMNOPQR
STUVWXYZ
abcdefghi
jklmnopq
rstuvwxyz
1234 5678
9 0

Journal on Paper Pizazz™ for a great look! Cutting out each letter separately and shadow-matting it makes a simple name special. The dash-and-dot outlines around the letters match those on the ducky mats and across the page. (The bathtub pattern is on page 139.)

Paper Pizazz™: *Baby* (duckies, bubbles)
Ducky cutouts: *Paper Pizazz™ Baby*
Page designer: Becky Goughnour and Katie Hacker for Hot Off The Press, Inc.

Green mats for rinds and teardrops punched from black paper for seeds turn plain red letters into chunks of watermelon.

Paper Pizazz™: *Ho Ho Ho* (Christmas plaid)
Watermelon stickers: Frances Meyer, Inc.®
Teardrop punch: Family Treasures
Page designer: LeNae Gerig and Becky Goughnour for Hot Off The Press, Inc.

The trick to using more than one patterned paper in your lettering is to put the papers together first. The wave paper was trimmed and glued onto the "handmade" paper, then the letters were traced and outlined. Each word was cut out and double matted as a single piece. The fancy "beaded" edge on the photo mats was made by turning the scallop scissors upside down to cut the inner mat.

Paper Pizazz™: *Bright Great Backgrounds, Solid Muted Colors*
Sand bucket cutout: *Paper Pizazz™ Childhood*
Decorative scissors: scallop by Fiskars®, Inc.
Page designer: Becky Goughnour for Hot Off The Press, Inc.

ABCDEFGHIJKLM
NOPQRSTUVWXYZ
abcdefghijklmnop
qrstuvwxyz
1234567890

The buttons and bows on the baptismal gown are the inspiration for the "buttons and bows" alphabet used for the headline on this page. It's just block outline lettering, rounded off a bit and embellished with little bows and stitches, but what a special look! Use this style on plain or patterned Paper Pizazz™.

Paper Pizazz™: *Holidays & Seasons* (embossed hearts), *Baby* (nursery items)
Rattle die cut: Ellison® Craft & Design
Decorative scissors: scallop by Fiskars®, Inc.
Page designer: Becky Goughnour for Hot Off The Press, Inc.

Italic Calligraphy

This lettering takes a special pen and a little practice, but it's easy to learn and has a very special look which adapts well to more formal or vintage-look pages. Use a fountain pen with a broad, flat nib or a chisel-tip felt pen designed for calligraphy; the size of the tip determines the size of the letters. Hold the pen so the tip stays at the same angle all the time—that's what creates the shaded look—and make the strokes in the directions indicated by the arrows. Practice on lined paper, then draw light pencil guidelines on your page to help keep your final lettering even.

a b c d e f g h i j k l m
n o p q r s t u v w x y z

A B C D E F G H I J K L M
N O P Q R S T U V W X Y Z

a b c d e f g h i j k l m n
o p q r s t u v
w x y z 1 2 3
4 5 6 7 8 9 0

Select a single photo, mat it on elegant papers and journal in calligraphy on a wide plain mat to create a formal setting that would be perfect as the introductory page in a wedding album. The gold vines and photo mats pick up the glint of the rings.

Paper Pizazz™: *Pretty Papers* (green marble), *Black & White Photos, Metallic Papers*
Leaf cutouts: *Paper Pizazz™ Embellishments*
Calligraphy pen: Pigma Callipen by Sakura
Gold pen: Zig® by EK Success Ltd.
Page designer: Becky Goughnour for Hot Off The Press, Inc.

CRISS CROSS

Straight pen lines that cross at the ends form an angular alphabet that could be used with an oriental theme as well as for a rustic country page.

For a ranch look that goes well with the varied textures of the wood paper, pasture grass and fencing, use a broad brown pen to "brand" the lettering on the wood.

Paper Pizazz™: *Country* (barnwood)
Brown paint pen: Zig® by EK Success Ltd.
Page designer: Allison Meyers for Memory Lane

ABCDEFGHIJK
LMNOPQRSTU
VWXYZ abcde
fghijklmnopqrstu
vwxyz1234567890

Thick & Thin Styles

ABCDEFGHI
JKLMNOPQR
STUVWXYZ
1234567890

ABCDEF
GHIJKLM
NOPQRST
UVWXYZ

Similar to old-fashioned "woodcut" letters, these alphabets also begin with stick letters. Thicken some strokes (like the upper alphabet) or draw heavier strokes parallel to them (bottom alphabet) to create an effect that is suitable for vintage or old-west pages. Fill in letters with patterned papers (page 111), or draw simple line figures inside each letter to reinforce the theme of your page.

The historic charm of an antebellum city is captured not only in these photos, but in the choice of letters, edge finishes and the antique leather look of the background paper.

Paper Pizazz™: *Black & White Photos* (crushed suede)
Title plaque: *Paper Pizazz™ Embellishments*
Fleur-de-lis punch: Family Treasures
Decorative scissors: mini antique by Family Treasures, colonial by Fiskars®, Inc
Page designer: Becky Goughnour for Hot Off The Press, Inc.

Cute, but it must take forever to fit those shapes inside the letters, right? Wrong! Trace the letters onto the patterned paper first, then cut out the shapes, glue them onto your page and draw the lines around them. Easy! Journal additional information on wide photo mats.

Paper Pizazz™: *Vacation* (pine trees)
Wildlife viewing area cutout: *Paper Pizazz™ Vacation*
Decorative scissors: volcano by Fiskars®, Inc.
Page designers: Becky Goughnour and Katie Hacker for Hot Off The Press, Inc.

ABCDEFGH
IJKLMNOPQ
RSTUVWX
YZ1234567890

Specialized Alphabets

These lettering styles are not for every page, but are worth the extra effort where they suit. Draw them directly on background paper (Bailey), cut out and mat a headline (Duchess), or cut and mat each letter separately (Chisaki).

ABCDEFGHIJKLMNOPQ
RSTUVWXYZ abcdefghijklm
nopqrstuvwxyz 1234567890

Rope lettering: Equally suitable for a western, a nautical or a camping theme, this clever style is worth the little practice it takes to master. Match it to rope frames drawn on ½" wide mats with a pattern stencil, then cut out.

Paper Pizazz™: *Country* (blue & tan check)
Apple cutouts: *Paper Pizazz™ Country*
Rope template:
  StenSource
  International, Inc.
Brown pen: Zig® by
  EK Success Ltd.
Page designers: LeNae
  Gerig and Becky
  Goughnour for Hot
  Off The Press, Inc.

Spiral lettering: This whimsical style is easier than it looks; it's so freeform, you really can't make a mistake! Draw pawprints on the mat to echo the background paper and provide journaling room.

Paper Pizazz™: *Pets*
Brown, white pens: Zig® by EK Success, Inc.
Decorative scissors: bow tie by Fiskars®, Inc.
Page designers: LeNae Gerig and Becky Goughnour for Hot Off The Press, Inc.

A sense of passing time is created by cropping and matting each photo in a circle, then arranging them in a bigger circle to resemble a clock face. Minimal journaling is needed, since the photos tell such a complete story.

Paper Pizazz™: *Black & White Photos* (black & white swirl)
Flower, corner punches: Family Treasures
Decorative scissors: ripple by Fiskars®, Inc.
Silver pen: Marvy® Uchida
Page designer: Becky Goughnour for Hot Off The Press, Inc.

Die Cuts to Delight

A staple of memory albums is die cuts. Ellison® Craft & Design's machine is shown in the photo on the left. It is easy to use and has interchangable dies. The beauty of the machine is that you can cut whatever shape you want out of whatever paper you like. While specialty stores often carry die cut machines, they are not availble to everyone, everywhere. So, we are grateful that Ellison® allows Hot Off The Press to give patterns for any dies we show in this book. Their in-house designer (and company vice-president) even created some of the album pages in this section. Thank you, Ellison®. And thank you, Sandi.

While die cuts are traditionally made of plain colored paper, when designs are cut of patterned Paper Pizazz™ you get some great looks as shown in this chapter. In addition, photos can be die cut (see page 116). And if you cut the same die out of several paper colors, you can cut them apart to decorate the basic cut (see page 120, where the crayons and pencils have been "dressed" with other papers). This technique was also used on the top of page 57 to put red shirts on yellow paper punched bears.

We can create scenes with die cuts as shown on the bottom of page 124 and the top of page 125. Of course, any of the techniques in this section will work with die cuts from other companies, and sometimes you can find die cuts in packages by theme. It's clear, die cuts are great placed on Paper Pizazz™ or cut out of Paper Pizazz™, or both!

This chapter's background paper is from *Paper Pizazz™ Bright Great Backgrounds*.

CALEB FIRST GRADE

caleb was so excited about his first day of school... he got up 2 hours early!

SEPTEMBER 3, 1997

Die cut your photos! Use a shaped die to cut a photo into a pattern that fits the theme of the page—like this apple. The apple was then matted with a narrow contoured border which matches the color of the small apple punch.

Paper Pizazz™: *School Days* (I can draw)
School bus, crayon cutouts: *Paper Pizazz™ School Days*
Large apple die cut: Ellison® Craft & Design
Small apple punch: Marvy® Uchida
Decorative scissors: zipper by Fiskars®, Inc.
Red paint pen: Zig® by EK Success Ltd.
Page designer: LeNae Gerig for Hot Off The Press, Inc.

© & ™ Ellison® Craft & Design

These fish and snorkeling photos were die cut into fish shapes. A school of smaller fish die cut from solid bright colors provide space for journaling.

Paper Pizazz™: *Bright Great Backgrounds*
Large, small fish die cuts: Ellison® Craft & Design
Decorative scissors: wave by Fiskars®, Inc.
Page designer: LeNae Gerig for Hot Off The Press

© & ™ Ellison® Craft & Design

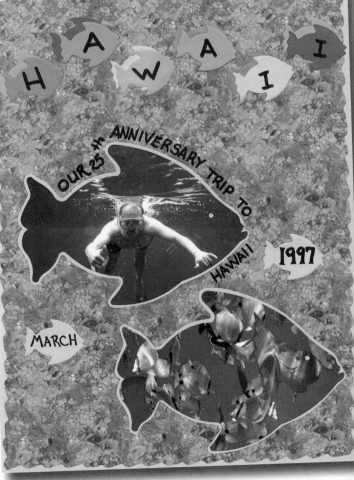

HAWAII

OUR 25th ANNIVERSARY TRIP TO HAWAII

1997

MARCH

Lettering with die cuts: Letters cut from pine-bough patterned paper headline this page. Double-matting the letters and photos adds texture to the page. A tree die cut from solid green and tucked partly behind the lower photo fills an awkward empty space meaningfully.

Paper Pizazz™: *Christmas* (pine boughs, white dot on green), *Ho Ho Ho* (red/green stripe)
Red alphabet stickers: Frances Meyer, Inc.®
Tree, alphabet die cuts: Ellison® Craft & Design
Page designer: Ann Smith for Memory Lane

© & ™ Ellison® Craft & Design

garrett & Dad
Picked out the
Perfect tree!
12-96

EGG HUNT
1996

Die cuts can be used to show motion. The photos were cropped into egg shapes and matted on pastel papers. The matted photos and Easter-theme die cuts were then layered to create a scene which has the effect of movement. (The bunny pattern is on page 57.)

Paper Pizazz™: *Holidays & Seasons* (Easter eggs), *Pets* (grass)
¼" round punch: McGill, Inc.
Bunny, basket, small egg die cuts: Ellison® Craft & Design
Decorative scissors: ripple by Fiskars®, Inc.
Page designer: LeNae Gerig for Hot Off The Press, Inc.

© & ™ Ellison® Craft & Design

BULLWINKLE

This is the Moose Dad shot. You named it Bullwinkle. 1992 Moose Hunt

You can even mat a die cut. The die-cut moose and tree repeat elements from the photos which also appear on the background paper. Woodsy colors and simple straight-cut mats contribute to the rustic look of this page.

Paper Pizazz™: *Great Outdoors* (moose & deer)
Moose, tree die cuts: Accu/Cut® Systems
Alphabet stickers: Frances Meyer, Inc.®
Page designer: Ann Smith for Memory Lane

© & ™ Ellison® Craft & Design

Snowflakes on top of snowflakes! The die cut snowflake and snowman were layered over the photos and background. A template was used to cut the "SNOW!" letters from snowflake-patterned paper, then they were layered on a darker snowflake paper. The variegated snow paper was also used to mat the center photo. The different shades of blue work well together.

Paper Pizazz™: *Holidays & Seasons, Quick & Easy*
Snowflake, snowman die cuts: Ellison® Craft & Design
Letter template: D.O.T.S.™
Page designer: Ann Smith for Memory Lane

© & ™ Ellison® Craft & Design

garrett was amazed to discover SNOW!! He played and rolled in the snow until half frozen 11-96

Use die cuts for framing, too. Here a special photo takes center stage with a frame made of overlapped hearts, each die cut from a different patterned paper.

Paper Pizazz™: *Christmas* (pine boughs, red tartan, red & green stripe), *Ho Ho Ho* (ho ho ho, Christmas plaid, red & white stripes, red & green dots)
Heart die cuts: Ellison® Craft & Design
Gold pen: Marvy® Uchida
Page designer: LeNae Gerig for Hot Off The Press, Inc.

© & ™ Ellison® Craft & Design

PUPPY LOVE

5-97

Another frame of overlapped hearts gets extra depth from using foam dots to lift some elements above the page. Only two patterned papers were used, since the heart sizes and pop-out effect provided sufficient variety.

Paper Pizazz™: *Ho Ho Ho* (white dot on red, red & white stripes)
Banner, heart die cuts: Ellison® Craft & Design
¼" red heart stickers, border: ©Mrs. Grossman's Paper Company
Red pen: Marvy® Uchida
Silver pen: Zig® by EK Success Ltd.
Alphabet stickers: Ellison® Craft & Design
Self-adhesive foam dots: All Night Media®, Inc.
Page designer: Sandi Genovese for Ellison® Craft & Design

© & ™ Ellison® Craft & Design

SCHOOL SNAP SHOTS

CHERYL 10

STACEY 8

SEAN 12

KIMMY 6

Clever photo frames are created from simple rectangular mats, turned into clipboards with die-cut tops. The school theme is reinforced with primary colors and crayon die cuts. The crayons were "dressed" with patterned and solid papers—each was cut from three colors, then the unwanted areas were trimmed away and the die cuts were layered for a realistic-looking crayon.

Paper Pizazz™: *Christmas* (white dot on green), *Ho Ho Ho* (white dot on red), *Birthday* (colorful stripes)
Crayon, clipboard die cuts: Ellison® Craft & Design
Star stickers: ©Mrs. Grossman's Paper Company
Red alphabet stickers: Making Memories™
Black alphabet stickers: C-Thru® Ruler Co.
Page designer: Sandi Genovese for Ellison® Craft & Design

These plaid pencils use the same "dressing" technique as the crayons on the page above. White colored pencil on black paper creates the look of a chalkboard. The central photo was lifted off the page with adhesive foam dots to give it greater impact.

Paper Pizazz™: *School Days* (yellow pad, school tartan)
Apple, pencil die cuts: Ellison® Craft & Design
White pencil: Berol Prismatic
Self-adhesive foam dots: All Night Media®, Inc.
Page designer: Sandi Genovese for Ellison® Craft & Design

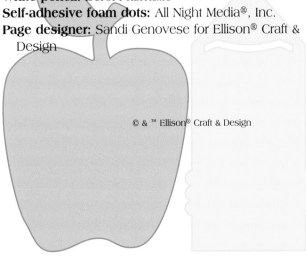

School Days

You can quilt with die cuts! The frame and heart are one all die. Cut it from white paper, glue the photo behind the heart and line the other openings with dotted paper. Mat on red and glue to a white background sheet. Lettering and a heart die cut from the dotted paper are matted to match. To keep the page from being too perfect to be interesting, add hand-drawn red stitching lines and an off-center heart sticker.

Paper Pizazz™: *Ho Ho Ho* (white dot on red)
Alphabet, quilt, heart die cuts: Ellison® Craft & Design
Small heart sticker: ©Mrs. Grossman's Paper Co.
Red pen: Marvy® Uchida
Page designer: Sandi Genovese for Ellison® Craft & Design

The same die cut from red paper, without embellishment.

Another quilt block die cut is perfect for a grouping of five related photos. The lettering was die cut and mounted on solid red to match the matted block, then embellished with random dots made with an acid-free red pen. This "five-minute page" is about as easy as it gets!

Paper Pizazz™: *Birthday* (colorful stripes)
Alphabet, quilt die cuts: Ellison® Craft & Design
Red pen: Zig® by EK Success Ltd.
Page designer: Sandi Genovese for Ellison® Craft & Design

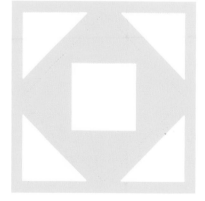

The same die cut from yellow paper, without embellishment.

Die cuts were used here to show motion. Die-cut balloons and noisemakers were layered for action. Foam dots raise the unmatted photo, some balloons and the centers of the noisemakers off the page. (The balloon patterns are on page 142.)

Paper Pizazz™: *Birthday* (colorful stripes), *Ho Ho Ho* (red & white stripes, white dot on red), *Christmas* (white dot on green)
Noisemaker, balloon die cuts: Ellison® Craft & Design
Border stickers: ©Mrs. Grossman's Paper Co.
Alphabet stickers: Making Memories™
Self-adhesive foam dots: All Night Media®, Inc.
Page designer: Sandi Genovese for Ellison® Craft & Design

Use die cuts to duplicate a patterned paper's theme. The rose was die cut from both grass and solid dark yellow paper, then the two die cuts were trimmed and layered. A ¼" strip was cut from each edge of the rose paper to form the border of the right page. The remainder of the sheet makes a "fat mat" for the left photo. (The rose pattern is on page 103.)

Paper Pizazz™: *Pets* (grass), *Romantic Papers*
Rose, picture frames, lettering die cuts: Ellison® Craft & Design
Heart stickers: ©Mrs. Grossman's Paper Co.
Silver pen: Zig® by EK Success Ltd.
Page designer: Sandi Genovese for Ellison® Craft & Design

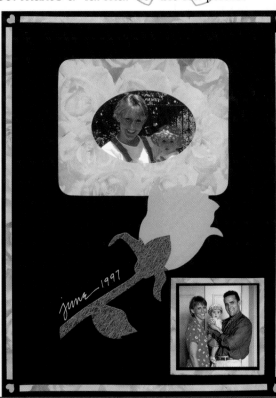

A black background really makes the colors of these pages stand out. The clear keepsake envelope was die cut from a page protector and used to hold dried petals from the wedding bouquet. (The large rose pattern is on page 103.)

Paper Pizazz™:
Holidays &
Seasons (roses)
Rose, gift card
envelope,
Congrats die
cuts: Ellison®
Craft & Design
Heart stickers:
©Mrs.
Grossman's
Paper Co.
Page designer:
Sandi
Genovese for
Ellison® Craft
& Design

Frame with die cuts! Snapshots from school plays, etc. often contain too many people and too much distracting background. Silhouette the subject, then mount on a white background inside a frame to focus on your special people. Here the antlers were allowed to bump out of the frame for a three-dimensional effect.

Paper Pizazz™: *Ho Ho Ho* (red & white stripes),
Romantic Papers
Ornament die cuts: Ellison® Craft & Design
Heart sticker: ©Mrs. Grossman's Paper Co.
Page designer: Sandi Genovese for Ellison® Craft
& Design

© & ™ Ellison® Craft & Design

HOME GROWN

CHRIS

JOSH

ADAMS

SERINA

Homegrown indeed! Die-cut seed packets on wooden stakes frame family faces in a colorful way. The carrots were cut from orange paper and lined with an orange pen; green tops were cut separately and glued on. (If die cuts are not available, enlarge the small seed packet pattern to 5" tall for the large packet).

Paper Pizazz™: *Pets* (grass), *Ho Ho Ho* (white dot on red), *Country* (barnwood)
⅜" alphabet stickers: Ellison® Craft & Design
¼" alphabet stickers: C-Thru® Ruler Co.
Carrot, seed packet die cuts: Ellison® Craft & Design
Orange pen: Marvy® Uchida
Ladybug stickers: ©Mrs. Grossman's Paper Company
Page designer: Sandi Genovese for Ellison® Craft & Design

carrot, seed packet © & ™ Ellison® Craft & Design

daisy, butterfly © & ™ Ellison® Craft & Design

Create a scene with die cuts! The center of these sunflowers is the perfect place to feature various views of a sweet face, awake and asleep. The flower die cuts and realistic wooden fence combine to create a wonderful garden, set in a perfect blue sky. (The sunflower and iris patterns are on page 141. Cut a butterfly die cut in half to make a side view.)

Paper Pizazz™: *Christmas* (white dot on green), *Country* (barnwood), *Vacation* (clouds)
Flower, alphabet, butterfly die cuts: Ellison® Craft & Design
Bug stickers: ©Mrs. Grossman's Paper Co.
Page designer: Sandi Genovese for Ellison® Craft & Design

SHAYA M.

REES

hyacinth, tulip © & ™ Ellison® Craft & Design

Die cuts reinforce the patterned papers. Die-cut snowflakes and mittens point up the important fact about this scene: It's cold! Notice the layered white paper at the bottom curves to resemble snowdrifts. The lower photo was trimmed to follow the curve and accentuate the journaling. (The open snowflake pattern is on page 118.)

Paper Pizazz™: *Christmas* (snowflakes)
Snowflakes, mitten die cuts: Ellison® Craft & Design
Rectangle punch: McGill, Inc.
Page designer: Brenda Birrell for Pebbles in My Pocket

Super simple and stunning—this page gets a lot of impact from just a few pastel dots, piled like tubby bubbles around the page. The colors of the bubbles, mats and letters were taken from the background paper.

Paper Pizazz™: *Baby* (bubbles)
Circle, alphabet die cuts: ©Pebbles in My Pocket
¼" round punch: McGill, Inc.
Computer typeface: D.J. Inkers™
Page designer: Launa Naylor for Pebbles in My Pocket

125

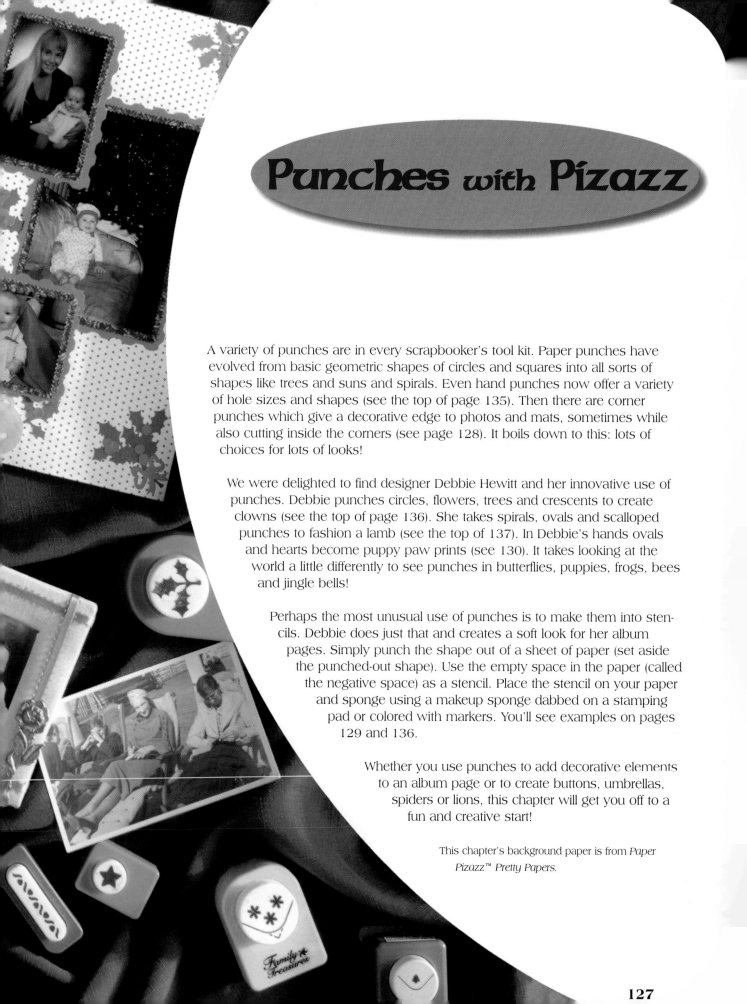

Punches with Pizazz

A variety of punches are in every scrapbooker's tool kit. Paper punches have evolved from basic geometric shapes of circles and squares into all sorts of shapes like trees and suns and spirals. Even hand punches now offer a variety of hole sizes and shapes (see the top of page 135). Then there are corner punches which give a decorative edge to photos and mats, sometimes while also cutting inside the corners (see page 128). It boils down to this: lots of choices for lots of looks!

We were delighted to find designer Debbie Hewitt and her innovative use of punches. Debbie punches circles, flowers, trees and crescents to create clowns (see the top of page 136). She takes spirals, ovals and scalloped punches to fashion a lamb (see the top of 137). In Debbie's hands ovals and hearts become puppy paw prints (see 130). It takes looking at the world a little differently to see punches in butterflies, puppies, frogs, bees and jingle bells!

Perhaps the most unusual use of punches is to make them into stencils. Debbie does just that and creates a soft look for her album pages. Simply punch the shape out of a sheet of paper (set aside the punched-out shape). Use the empty space in the paper (called the negative space) as a stencil. Place the stencil on your paper and sponge using a makeup sponge dabbed on a stamping pad or colored with markers. You'll see examples on pages 129 and 136.

Whether you use punches to add decorative elements to an album page or to create buttons, umbrellas, spiders or lions, this chapter will get you off to a fun and creative start!

This chapter's background paper is from *Paper Pizazz™ Pretty Papers.*

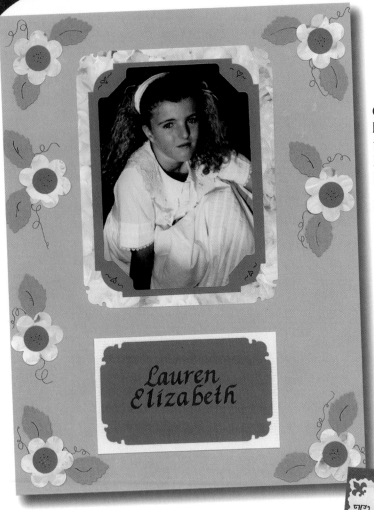

Combinations of punches can be used to build a scene. These flowers are pretty by themselves, but with the addition of green leaves, centers and hand-drawn details they become a flower garden to frame this portrait.

Paper Pizazz™: *Pretty Papers* (cream roses)
Corner punches: Victorian, corner frame by All Night Media®, Inc.
Flower, leaf, ½" circle punches: Family Treasures
Calligraphy pen: Pigma Callipen by Sakura
Page designer: Ann Smith for Memory Lane

Punches do double duty on this page. The fleur-de-lis are punched out of the corners of the ivory mats and glued as embellishments for the purple mat and the right-hand page corners.

Paper Pizazz™: *Pretty Papers* (jewel colors)
Fleur-de-lis corner punch: Family Treasures
Corner punch: corner rounder by Fiskars®, Inc.
Decorative scissors: ripple by Fiskars®, Inc.
Page designer: Anne-Marie Spencer for Hot Off The Press, Inc.

Punches do double duty in a different way here—the large flower punch and spiral punch were used to make stencils (see page 127). Sponging gives a watercolor effect. For a variety of colors, use felt markers directly on the sponge.

Paper Pizazz™: *Bright Great Backgrounds*
⅜" flower, border, ⅛" round punches: McGill, Inc.
Spiral punch: All Night Media®, Inc.
1¼" flower punch: Family Treasures
Colored markers: Zig® by EK Success Ltd.
Ink pads: ColorBox®
Decorative scissors: mini pinking by Fiskars®, Inc.
Page designer: Debbie Hewitt

Look imaginatively at your punches to see how they can be combined in creative ways. With punched-out wings and spiral antennae, flowers metamorphose into butterflies! The punched hearts add detail to the wings.

Paper Pizazz™: *Vacation* (clouds)
Alphabet stickers: Frances Meyer, Inc.®
Spiral punch: All Night Media®, Inc.
Flower, oval punches: Family Treasures
Heart punch: McGill, Inc.
Decorative scissors: scallop by Fiskars®, Inc.
Page designer: Debbie Hewitt

Spiral centers and fantasy colors create whimsical outline flowers, which were first cut with a flower punch. An oval punch was then used to cut out the inside of each flower petal and to make the leaves.

Paper Pizazz™: *Pretty Papers* (purple sponged)
Spiral punch: All Night Media®, Inc.
Flower, oval punches: Family Treasures
Decorative scissors: cloud by Fiskars®, Inc.
Page designer: Debbie Hewitt

To coordinate with the pawprint paper, punched pawprints made with hearts and circles adorn the mats of these photos and reveal the brown of the mats. Larger hearts combined with ovals make giant prints to fill empty areas of the page. The large heart was also used to make a bone template: Punch it twice with the points 1" apart, then cut a ⅜" strip connecting the points.

Paper Pizazz™: *Pets*
⅛" round, ¼" and ⅞" heart punches: McGill, Inc.
Oval punch: Family Treasures
Decorative scissors: mini pinking, deckle by Fiskars®, Inc.
Page designer: Debbie Hewitt

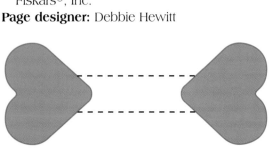

"Bee" creative to get the most use from your punches. The scalloped oval was used for the bee bodies (glue the black stripes onto the yellow paper before punching). Yellow hearts form wings, a yellow circle makes the head and two black spirals are antennae. The same scalloped oval, punched and trimmed as shown, becomes a beehive.

Paper Pizazz™: *Country* (wire & daisies)
Spiral punch: All Night Media®, Inc.
Scalloped oval, ½" round punches: Family Treasures
⅜" oval, heart punches: McGill, Inc.
Page designer: Debbie Hewitt

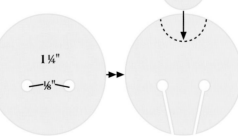

Round punches in a variety of sizes are among the most versatile tools in your scrapbooking kit. Four sizes of circles were used to make these jingle bells; the holly berries are also simple circles.

Paper Pizazz™: *Ho Ho Ho* (red & green dots), *Christmas* (holly)
Bow, leaf, ⅛", ¼" round punches: McGill, Inc.
½", 1¼" round punches: Family Treasures
Number stickers: Frances Meyer, Inc.®
Decorative scissors: zipper, mini pinking by Fiskars®, Inc.
Page designer: Debbie Hewitt

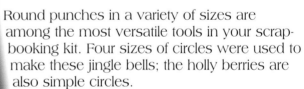

Decorated trees are everywhere on this page. The large cut-out tree was matted and adorned with two sizes of stars. The small stars also top the trees punched around the white mats; round punches in the paper of the green mats reveal the red lining paper behind.

Paper Pizazz™: *Christmas*
Star, tree, ⅛" round punches: McGill, Inc.
Page designer: Debbie Hewitt

When is a sun a spider? When it's punched from black paper, it's top and bottom rays are cut off, and it's decorated with white dots for eyes! Use a fine pen to draw the silk lines.

Paper Pizazz™: *Holidays & Seasons* (candy corn)
Halloween cutout: *Paper Pizazz™ Embellishments*
Small sun punch: McGill, Inc.
White pens: Zig® by EK Success Ltd.
Page designer: Debbie Hewitt

What a beautiful example of decorative matting! The yellow mat was trimmed to match the photo, then the scissors were turned over to trim the outer blue mat, creating a scalloped diamond effect. The puppy faces begin with inverted 1¼" white hearts. The face details are punched, then matching black hearts are glued to the backs. The ears are ⅞" brown hearts cut in half.

Paper Pizazz™: *Light Great Backgrounds*
Alphabet stickers: Making Memories™
⅞" and 1¼" hearts, bow, ¹⁄₁₆" and ⅛" round, puppy nose **(shape E) punches:** McGill, Inc.
Oval punch: Family Treasures
Decorative scissors: seagull by Fiskars®, Inc.
Page designer: Debbie Hewitt

trimmed and punched balloon for pig face

More animal faces! The lion uses spiral, oval, ¼" round and heart punches. The pig is assembled from balloon, oval, ½" round and spiral punches. The frog is made with the flower, heart and bow punches. The punched shapes were lined with matching black shapes where necessary to prevent other layers from showing through (for example, a black balloon behind the pink balloon to make the pig's eyes black and hide the base of the ears). Each animal was glued to a photo, then the photo was silhouette matted to include the animal shape.

Paper Pizazz™: *Country* (barnwood)
Heart; outline, solid bows; ¹⁄₁₆", ⅛", ¼" round punches: McGill, Inc.
Flower, oval, ½" round, balloon punches: Family Treasures
Spiral punch: All Night Media®, Inc.
Page designer: Debbie Hewitt

Consider the "negative spaces" of your punches. The same scalloped oval punch used for the bees and hives on page 131 was used here to cut away half circles to make the umbrella tops (see below). Tip: Cut the scallops first, then position the circle punch over the negative space to punch the umbrella. Cut the handles from solid red paper.

Paper Pizazz™: *Child's Play* (raindrops)
Circle, scalloped oval, teardrop, cloud punches: Family Treasures
Alphabet stickers: Frances Meyer, Inc.®
Decorative scissors: jigsaw by Fiskars®, Inc.
Page designer: Debbie Hewitt

A plastic garbage bag is the only suitable garment for a kid surrounded by this much paint! The heart-shaped paint puddles on the palette match the heart punches around the matted photo, and the teardrop punches remind us of the bristles of a paintbrush. (The palette pattern is on page 140.)

Paper Pizazz™: *School Days* (splats)
Alphabet stickers: Frances Meyer, Inc.®
Teardrop, ¼" heart punches: McGill, Inc.
⅞" heart punch: Family Treasures
Palette die cut: Ellison® Craft & Design
Page designer: Debbie Hewitt

A different shadow effect is achieved by layering the sticker letters with the black on top rather than behind, popping the name forward off the page like a backlit sign. The coin background paper comments on the casino bucket the subject is wearing. Punched playing-card symbols and dice reinforce the casino theme.

Paper Pizazz™: *Book of Firsts*
¹⁄₁₆" **round, club, ¼" diamond, spade, ⅞" and ¼" heart punches:** McGill, Inc.
½" **square, ½" diamond punches:** Family Treasures
Alphabet stickers: Making Memories™
Decorative scissors: mini pinking, pinking by Fiskars®, Inc.
Page designer: Debbie Hewitt

It's easier to punch outline shapes when you punch the inner shape first, then center the punched area in the larger punch to cut the outside. Four star sizes were combined in different ways to create these varied looks (the bow punch was used to make tails for the shooting stars).

Paper Pizazz™: *Adult Birthday* (blue stars)
¼", ½", ⅞" and 1" **star punches, bow punches:** McGill, Inc.
Page designer: Debbie Hewitt

Note how careful alignment of the scissors on the three mats causes the yellow center mat to look like a chain border between the blue mats. Each clown head is another example of combining punches creatively: The hat is a yellow Christmas tree, the hair is two orange clouds and the collar is the bottom half of a yellow flower. The nose and pom poms are ¼" red circles. The eyes and mouth were punched in the face, which was lined with a matching 1¼" black circle so the features show black.

Paper Pizazz™: *Child's Play* (dots on purple), *Great Bright Backgrounds*
Christmas tree, ⅛" and ¼" round, crescent punches: McGill, Inc.
1¼" circle, rectangle, flower punches: Family Treasures
Alphabet stickers: Frances Meyer, Inc.®
Decorative scissors: zipper by Fiskars®, Inc.
Page designer: Debbie Hewitt

Multicolored balloons float among puffy clouds, all sponged onto a white background using stencils made with punches (see page 127). The balloons were decorated with smaller punched shapes, and a punched bow ties each group together with strings drawn by hand.

Paper Pizazz™: *Birthday* (colorful stripes, party hats)
1¼" round punch: Family Treasures
Balloon, bow, heart, flower, star punches: McGill, Inc.
Stamp pad ink: ColorBox®
Decorative scissors: jigsaw, mini scallop by Fiskars®, Inc.
Blue pen: Zig® by EK Success Ltd.
Page designer: Debbie Hewitt

These clever sleepytime sheep were assembled on a patterned background, then cut out and mounted on a cloud to coordinate with the cropped photos.

Paper Pizazz™: *Light Great Backgrounds, Disney's Every Day with Mickey & Friends*
Spiral punch: All Night Media®, Inc.
Oval, scalloped oval punch: Family Treasures
⅛" round punch: McGill, Inc.
½" round punch: Marvy® Uchida
Page designer: Debbie Hewitt

This "5-minute page" is also cute as a button! Round matted photos repeat the shapes of the buttons, which were made with punches. The polka-dot background paper is a perfect complement, and even the letters are decorated with dots.

Paper Pizazz™: *School Days* (colorful dots)
Pink alphabet stickers: Making Memories™
1⁄16", ⅛", ½" round punches: McGill, Inc.
1 ¼" round punch: Family Treasures
Pink, red pens: Zig® by EK Success Ltd.
Page designer: Debbie Hewitt

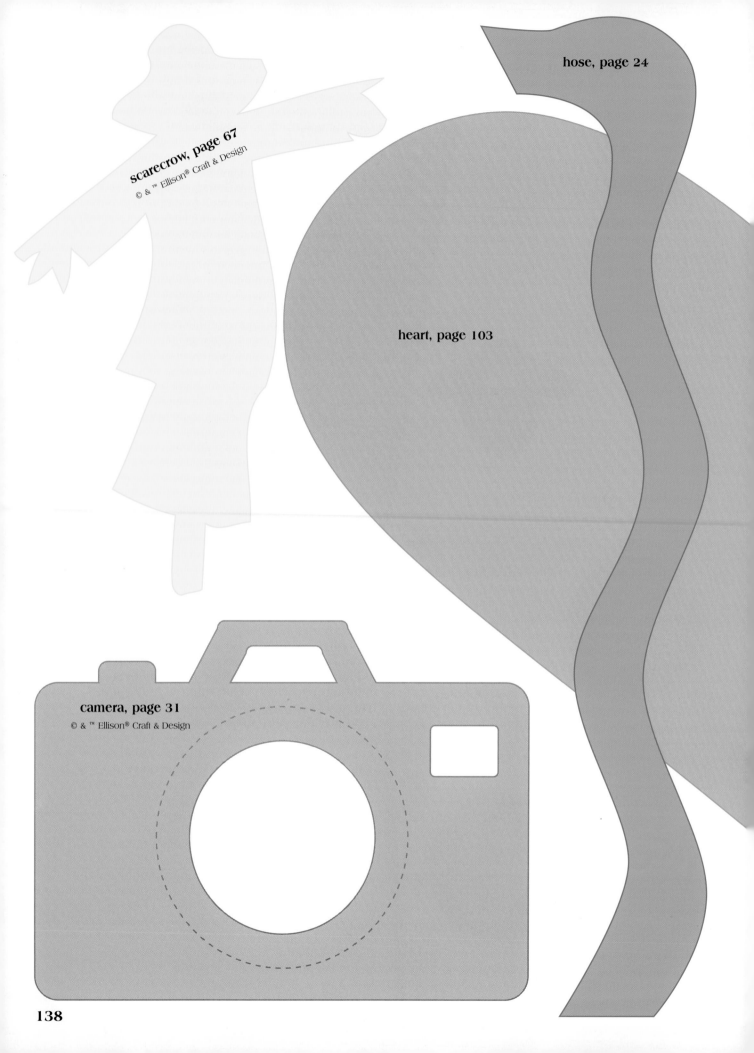

scarecrow, page 67
© & ™ Ellison® Craft & Design

hose, page 24

heart, page 103

camera, page 31
© & ™ Ellison® Craft & Design

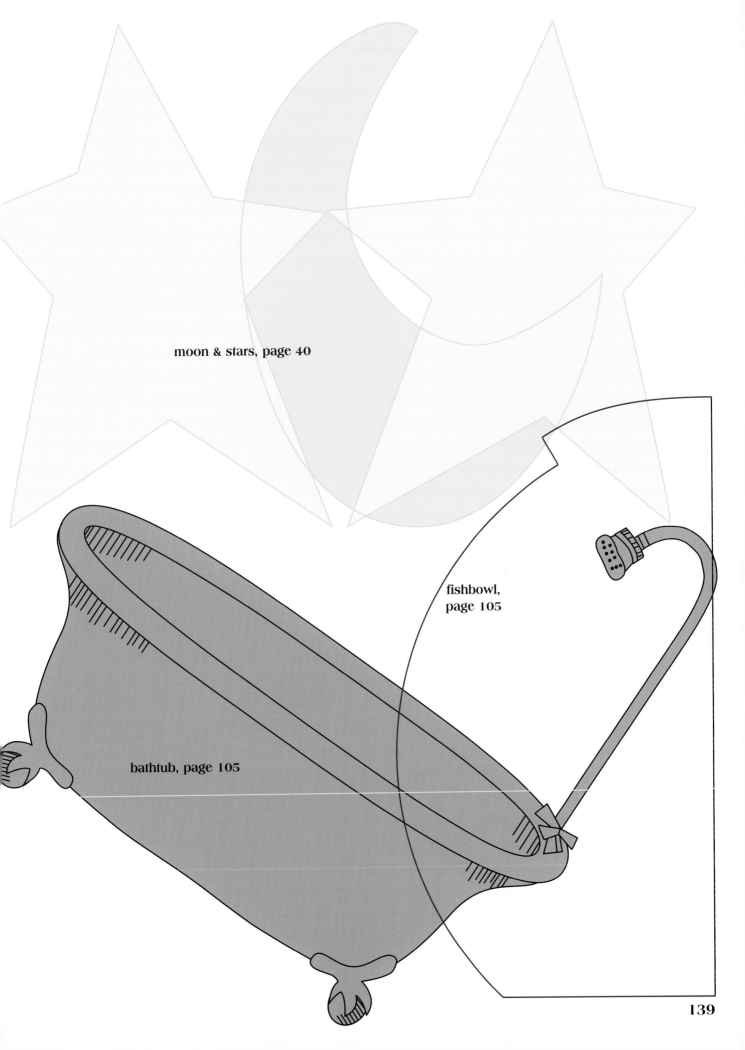

moon & stars, page 40

fishbowl,
page 105

bathtub, page 105

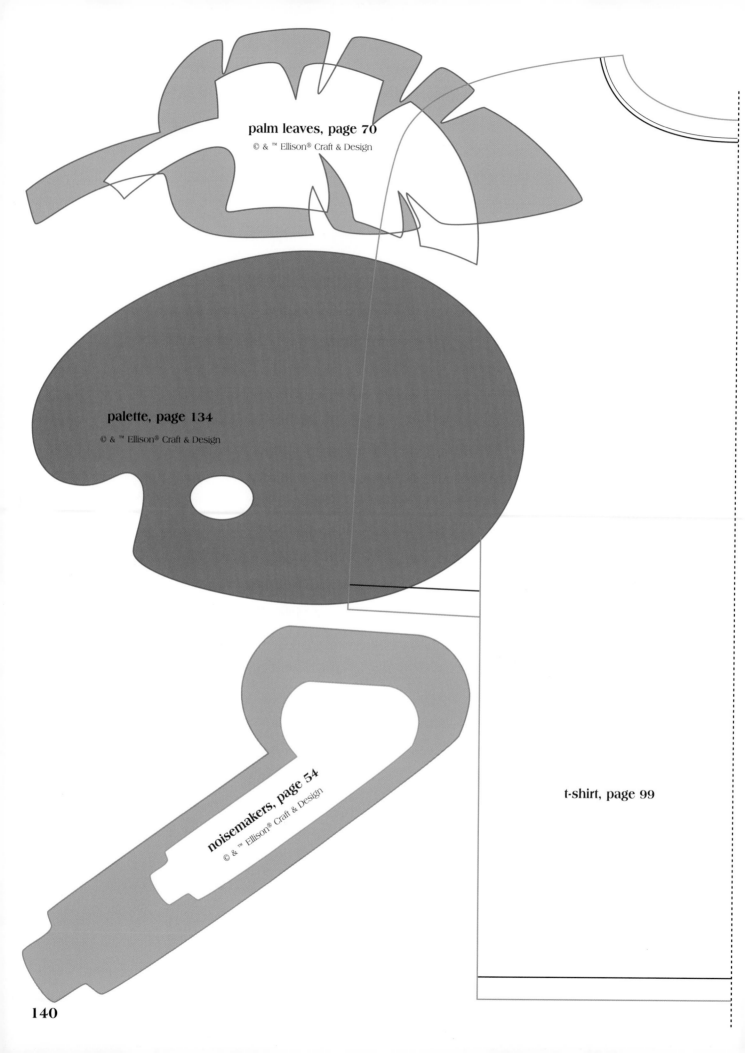

palm leaves, page 70

© & ™ Ellison® Craft & Design

palette, page 134

© & ™ Ellison® Craft & Design

noisemakers, page 54

© & ™ Ellison® Craft & Design

t-shirt, page 99

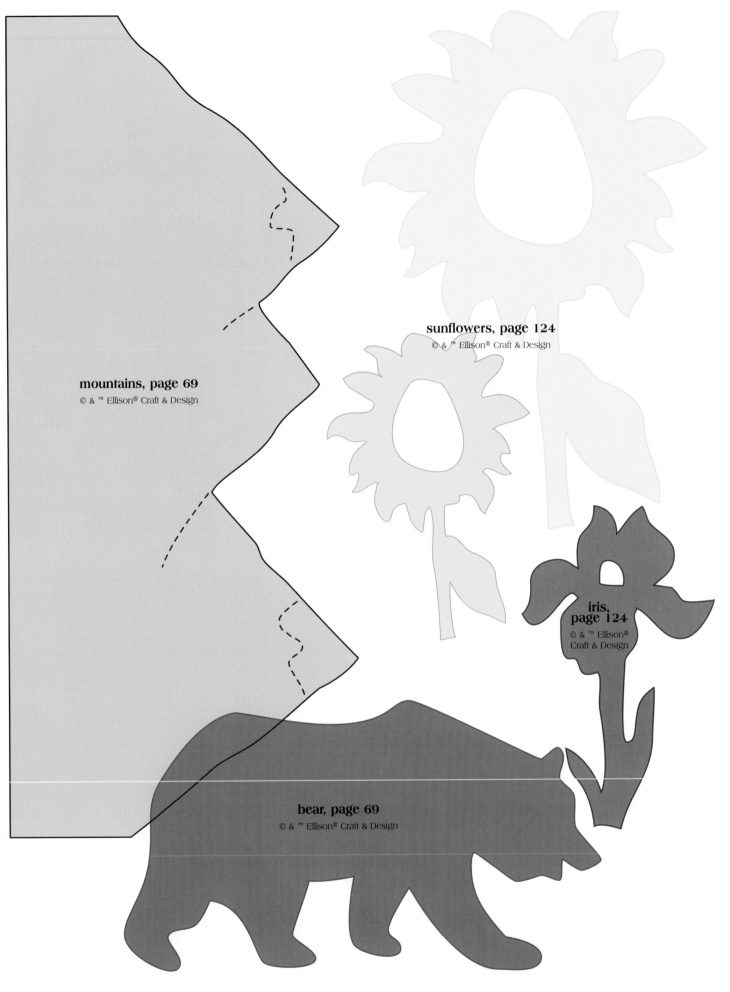

mountains, page 69
© & ™ Ellison® Craft & Design

sunflowers, page 124
© & ™ Ellison® Craft & Design

iris,
page 124
© & ™ Ellison®
Craft & Design

bear, page 69
© & ™ Ellison® Craft & Design

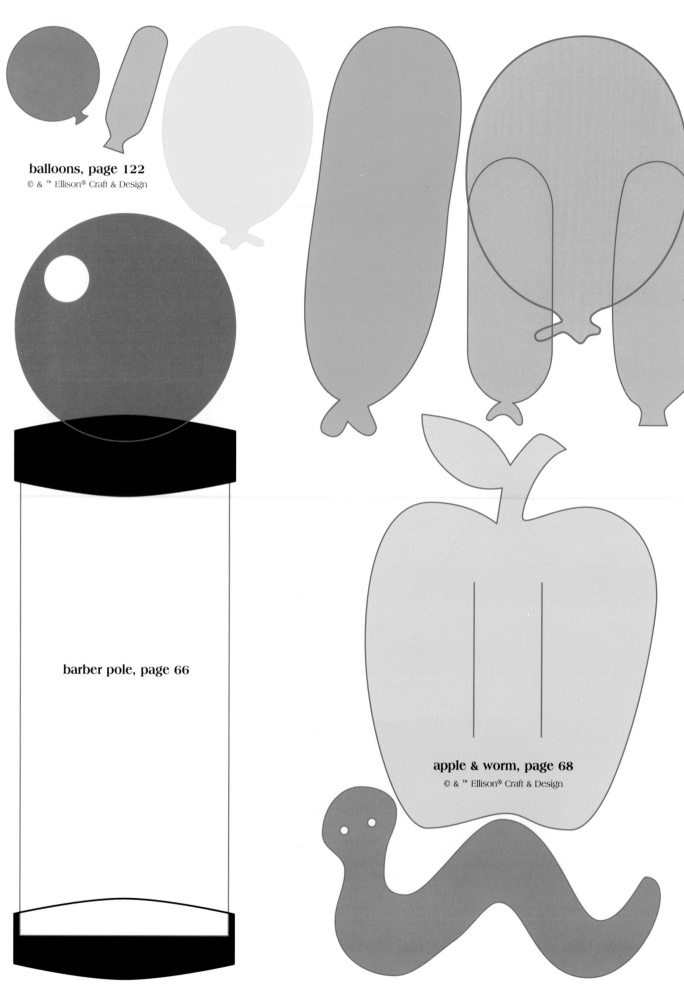

balloons, page 122
© & ™ Ellison® Craft & Design

barber pole, page 66

apple & worm, page 68
© & ™ Ellison® Craft & Design

Glossary:

Acid-free
Acid is used in paper manufacturing to break apart the wood fibers and the lignin which holds them together. If acid remains in the materials used for photo albums, the acid can react chemically with photographs and accelerate their deterioration. Acid-free products have a pH factor of 7 to 8.5. It's imperative that all materials (glue, pens, paper, etc.) used in memory albums or scrapbooks be acid-free.

Acid migration
is the transfer of acidity from one item to another through physical contact or acidic vapors. If a newspaper clipping were put into an album, the area it touched would turn yellow or brown. A de-acidification spray can be used on acidic papers, or they can be color photocopied onto acid-free papers.

Archival quality
is a term used to indicate materials which have undergone laboratory analysis to determine that their acidic and buffered content is within safe levels.

Buffered Paper
During manufacture a buffering agent such as calcium carbonate or magnesium bicarbonate can be added to paper to neutralize acid contaminants. Such papers have a pH of 8.5.

Cropping
Cutting or trimming a photo to keep only the most important parts. See page 10 for cropping ideas and information about cropping Polaroid photos.

Journaling
refers to the text on an album page giving details about the photographs. Journaling can be done in your own handwriting or with adhesive letters, rub-ons, etc. It is probably the most important part of memory albums. See pages 100–113 for more information.

Lignin
is the bonding material which holds wood fibers together as a tree grows. If lignin remains in the final paper product (as with newsprint) it will become yellow and brittle over time. Most paper other than newsprint is lignin-free.

pH factor
refers to the acidity of a paper. The pH scale is the standard for measurement of acidity and alkalinity. It runs from 0 to 14 with each number representing a ten-fold increase; pH neutral is 7. Acid-free products have a pH factor from 7 to 8.5. Special pH tester pens are available to help you determine the acidity or alkalinity of products.

Photo-safe
is a term similar to archival quality but more specific to materials used with photographs. Acid-free is the determining factor for a product to be labeled photo-safe.

Sheet protectors
These are made of plastic to slip over a finished album page. They can be side-loading or top-loading and fit 8½"x11" pages or 12"x12" sheets. It is important that they be acid-free. Polypropylene is commonly used—never use vinyl sheet protectors.

MANUFACTURERS & SUPPLIERS:

Accu/Cut® Systems
1035 E. Dodge St.
Fremont, NE 68025

All Night Media®, Inc.
Post Office Box 10607
San Rafael, CA 94912

American Traditional Stencils
442 First New Hampshire Tpk.
Northwood, NH 03261

Artifacts, Inc
Post Office Box 3399
Palestine, TX 75802

C-Thru® Ruler Co.
6 Britton Dr.
Bloomfield, CT 06002

Canson-Talens, Inc.
21 Industrial Dr.
S. Hadley, MA 01075

Chartpak®
One River Road
Leeds, MA 01053

ColorBox® by Clearsnap, Inc.
509 30th St.
Anacortes, WA 98221

D. J. Inkers™
Post Office Box 2462
Sandy, UT 84091

D.O.T.S.™
738 East Quality Dr
American Fork, UT 84003

Deja Views™ by C-Thru®
6 Britton Dr.
Bloomfield, CT 06002

EK Success Ltd.
611 Industrial Rd.
Carlstadt, NJ 07072

Ellison® Craft & Design
Toll Free 888-972-7238
714-724-0555

Extra Special Products Corp.
Post Office Box 777
Greenville, OH 45331

Family Treasures, Inc.
24922 Anza Dr., Unit D
Valencia, CA 91355

Fiskars®, Inc.
7811 W. Stewart Avenue
Wausau, WI 54401

Frances Meyer Inc.®
Post Office Box 3088
Savannah, GA 31402

Hot Off The Press, Inc.
1250 NW Third, Dept B
Canby, OR 97013
503-266-9102

Hygloss Products, Inc.
402 Broadway
Passaic, NJ 07055

Keeping Memories Alive™
260 N. Main
Spanish Fork, UT 84660

Lasting Impressions for
Paper, Inc.
585 W. 2600 S. Suite A
Bountiful, UT 84010

Making Memories™
Post Office Box 1188
Centerville, UT 84014

Marvy® Uchida
3535 Del Amo Blvd
Torrance, CA 90503

McGill, Inc.
Post Office Box 177
Marengo, IL 60152

Melissa Neufeld Inc.
6940 Koll Center Parkway, Suite 100
Pleasanton, CA 94566

Mrs. Grossman's Paper Company
Post Office Box 4467
Petaluma, CA 94955

Pebbles In My Pocket
1132 S. State St.
Orem, UT 84058

Provo Craft®
285 E. 900 South
Provo, UT 84606

Sakura of America
30780 San Clemente St.
Hayward, CA 94544

SandyLion Sticker Designs
400 Cochrane Dr.
Markham, Ontario L3R 8E3

SpotPen™
Post Office Box 1559
Las Cruces, NM 88004

StenSource International, Inc.
18971 Hess Avenue
Sonora, CA 95370

Stickopotamus™ by EK Success Ltd.
611 Industrial Rd.
Carlstadt, NJ 07072

Venus Decorative Ribbon
41-50 24th St.
Long Island City, NY 11101

RETAIL STORES:

Memory Lane
700 E. Southern Avenue
Mesa, AZ 85204

Pebbles In My Pocket
1132 S. State St.
Orem, UT 84058

SCRAPBOOK MAGAZINES:

Creating Keepsakes
888-247-5282

Memory Makers
800-366-6465